JUNIOR
READING EXPERT

A Theme-Based Reading Course for Young EFL Learners

Level 4

JUNIOR
READING EXPERT

Level 4

Series Editor	Ji-hyun Kim
Project Editors	Eun-kyung Kim, Jun-hee Kim, Yoon-joung Choi
Contributing Writers	Curtis Thompson, Bryce Olk, Angela Hai Yue Lan, Patrick Ferraro, MyAn Le, Keeran Murphy
Illustrators	Soo-hyeon Lee, Yoon-seo Jung, Mi-rae Shin, Sun-kyung Ha
Design	Hoon-jung Ahn, Ji-young Ki
Editorial Designer	Sun-hee Kim
ISBN	979-11-253-4043-0 53740
Photo Credits	www.shutterstock.com

INTRODUCTION

Junior Reading Expert is a four-level reading course for EFL readers, with special relevance for older elementary school students and junior high school students. Students will acquire not only reading skills but also knowledge of various contemporary and academic topics.

Features

Covers Dynamic, Contemporary Topics

Engaging topics, including culture, sports, and literature, are developed in an easy and interesting way to motivate students.

Expands Knowledge

Each unit is composed of two closely related readings under one topic heading. These readings allow students to explore the theme in depth.

Features Longer Passages

EFL students are seldom exposed to long reading passages and therefore tend to find them difficult. Compelling and well-developed passages designed specifically for EFL students will help them learn to handle longer passages with ease.

Presents Different Text Types of Passages

Reading passages are presented as articles, letters, debates, interviews, and novels. This helps students become familiarized with a variety of writing formats and styles through different genres of readings.

Provides Various Exercises for Reading Skills

All readings are accompanied by different types of tasks, such as multiple choice, matching, short answer, true/false, and fill-in-the-blank. These exercises are carefully designed to develop the following reading skills: understanding main ideas, identifying details, drawing inferences, and recognizing organizational structures.

Series Overview

Each level of *Junior Reading Expert* is composed of 20 units, with two related readings accompanying each unit. The number of words in each Reading 1 passage is as follows:

Level 1: 150−170 words
Level 2: 170−190 words
Level 3: 190−210 words
Level 4: 210−230 words

Format

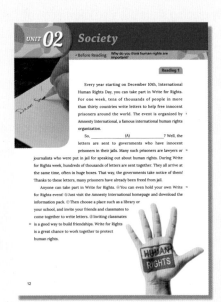

Reading 1

Reading 1 takes students into the first of the unit's two readings. Being the main reading of the unit, Reading 1 deals with various interesting and important topics in great depth. The passages gradually increase in difficulty as students progress through the book.

Different Types of Questions

A full page of different types of questions follows Reading 1. The questions concentrate on important reading skills, such as understanding the main idea, identifying details, drawing inferences, and recognizing the organizational structure.

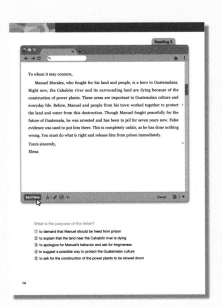

Reading 2

Reading 2 offers a second reading passage on the unit topic, the length of which is from 90 to 110 words. Reading 2 supplements Reading 1 with additional information, further explanation, or a new point of view.

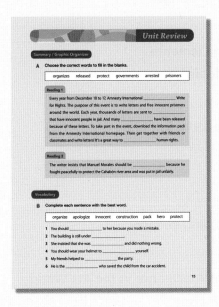

Unit Review

A Summary / Graphic Organizer
Either a summary or a graphic organizer is provided for Reading 1 and Reading 2 to facilitate a better understanding of the flow of passages. Performing this task also encourages the development of systematic comprehension skills.

B Vocabulary
Each unit is concluded with vocabulary practice. It checks students' knowledge of essential vocabulary words. Vocabulary practice requires students to either match definitions or choose words in context.

Table of Contents

Reading 1

The word "OK" is one of the most commonly used words in the world. Even though it's a fairly new word, its origin remained a mystery for many years. Some believed it came from the Greek word "*ola kala*", which means "all good." Others thought it came from the Native American 5 word "*okeh*." However, its true origin was finally revealed in the 1960s by a language scholar named Allen Read.

Read discovered that the word "OK" actually came from Charles Gordon Greene, the editor of The Boston Morning Post. In 1839, Greene created the word "OK" to make fun 10 of people with bad spelling. He joked that "OK" meant "oll korrect," which is an incorrect spelling of "all correct." Normally, weak jokes like this are quickly forgotten. However, the word "OK" got lucky.

In 1840, Martin Van Buren was running for reelection as the president of the United States. Because he grew up in a town called Kinderhook, he was given the 15 nickname "Old Kinderhook." ⓐ During his campaign, supporters shortened the nickname to "OK" and chanted "Vote for OK" at rallies. ⓑ Those days, all famous politicians had interesting nicknames. ⓒ They even started "O.K. Clubs" to support him. ⓓ As a result, "OK" spread through the United States, 20 and eventually the world.

These days, people have mostly forgotten about "Old Kinderhook." However, the word "OK" is still used to mean "all correct" as a way to agree with people.

1 **What is the passage mainly about?**

① why some words disappear

② ways to correct poor spelling

③ how people started to use "OK"

④ nicknames of American politicians

2 **Greene made up the word "OK" to** _____

_____ .

3 **It can be inferred from the underlined sentence that** _____ .

① the word "OK" was not forgotten

② the word "OK" has a short history

③ the word "OK" brings people luck

④ the word "OK" was loved by presidents

4 **Which sentence is NOT needed in the passage?**

① ⓐ   ② ⓑ   ③ ⓒ   ④ ⓓ

5 **What is NOT suggested in the passage?**

① The origin of "OK" had been unknown for a long time.

② "OK" actually originated from a Native American word.

③ "OK" was first used by the editor of The Boston Morning Post.

④ Martin Van Buren got his nickname because of his hometown.

6 **Write T if the statement is true and F if it's false.**

(1) Allen Read thought that the word "OK" came from a Greek word.

(2) The nickname of a politician made the word "OK" famous throughout the United States.

GOODBYE

We say the word "goodbye" for many reasons. But where is it from? The first known use of "goodbye" was written in a letter in 1573 by an English writer named Gabriel Harvey. However, he spelled it "godbwyes" and used it to mean "God be with you." At 5 that time, this was a common phrase. People couldn't communicate over long distances, so they would ask God to be with their loved ones when they said goodbye. Over time, however, people started saying "good" instead of "God," likely because of phrases like "good day" and "good evening." Also, as technology advanced, communication became easier, so the original meaning seemed less 10 necessary. But even though the meaning has changed, we still use "goodbye" to wish people well until we see them again.

What is the passage mainly about?

① how saying "goodbye" started and changed

② a writer who made common English phrases

③ the influence of communication on language

④ the history of using the word "God" in English

⑤ how the English spelling system has improved

Summary / Graphic Organizer

A Choose the correct words to fill in the blanks.

spread	origin	revealed	changed	supporters	spelling

Reading 1

No one knew the true _____ of the word "OK" until it was discovered by Allen Read. It is not from a Greek or Native American word, like some people thought. Instead, it was created to joke about people with bad _____ by incorrectly writing "all correct" as "oll korrect." "OK" gained popularity when an American politician ran for president again. Because he was nicknamed "Old Kinderhook," his _____ would often call him "OK." The word _____, and now it's a common way to agree with people!

Reading 2

The word "godbwyes" was first used in 1573 to mean "God be with you," but it _____ over time and became the word "goodbye."

Vocabulary

B Choose the correct word for each definition.

phrase	politician	history	origin	scholar	necessary	spell

1 the beginning or starting point of something: _____

2 a group of words that express a particular meaning or idea: _____

3 to speak or write the letters of a word in the right order: _____

4 the events of the past, especially from a certain period or country: _____

5 required for a specific purpose or to achieve a specific result: _____

6 someone with knowledge about a subject because they have studied it closely:

_____

Reading 1

Every year starting on December 10th, International Human Rights Day, you can take part in Write for Rights. For one week, tens of thousands of people in more than thirty countries write letters to help free innocent prisoners around the world. The event is organized by 5 Amnesty International, a famous international human rights organization.

So, _____(A)_____? Well, the letters are sent to governments who have innocent prisoners in their jails. Many such prisoners are lawyers or 10 journalists who were put in jail for speaking out about human rights. During Write for Rights week, hundreds of thousands of letters are sent together. They all arrive at the same time, often in huge boxes. That way, the governments take notice of them! Thanks to these letters, many prisoners have already been freed from jail.

Anyone can take part in Write for Rights. ⓐYou can even hold your own Write 15 for Rights event! ⓑJust visit the Amnesty International homepage and download the information pack. ⓒThen choose a place such as a library or your school, and invite your friends and classmates to come together to write letters. ⓓInviting classmates

20   is a good way to build friendships. Write for Rights is a great chance to work together to protect human rights.

1   **What is the best title for the passage?**

① Write a Letter to Help People!

② What Is Amnesty International?

③ How to Send an International Letter

④ Journalists' Efforts for Human Rights

2   **The purpose of Write for Rights is to** _____

_____ .

3   **What is the best choice for blank (A)?**

① what should you do if you get a letter

② when is the best time to write a letter

③ why do governments hate receiving letters

④ how can writing a letter free an innocent prisoner

4   **According to the passage, why are some lawyers and journalists in jail?**

① because they defended human rights

② because they accused innocent people

③ because they worked for other countries

④ because they gave money to government workers

5   **Which sentence is NOT needed in the passage?**

① ⓐ   ② ⓑ   ③ ⓒ   ④ ⓓ

6   **Which of the following is NOT mentioned about Write for Rights?**

① when it is held

② who organizes it

③ how it first started

④ how to start your own

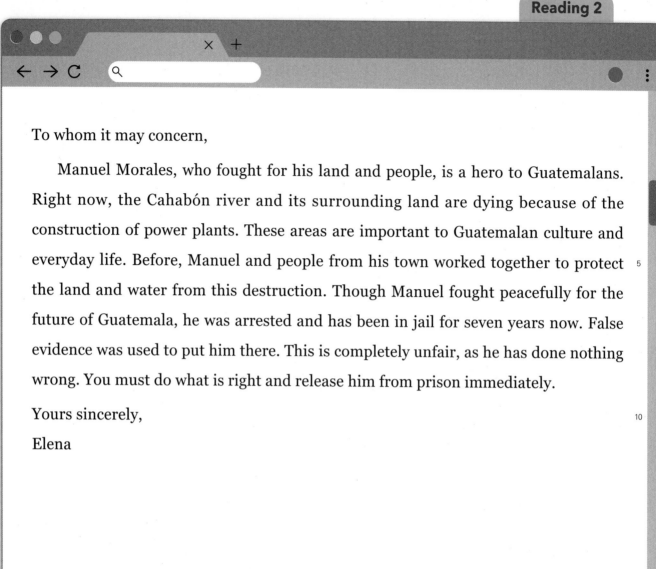

To whom it may concern,

Manuel Morales, who fought for his land and people, is a hero to Guatemalans. Right now, the Cahabón river and its surrounding land are dying because of the construction of power plants. These areas are important to Guatemalan culture and everyday life. Before, Manuel and people from his town worked together to protect ⁵ the land and water from this destruction. Though Manuel fought peacefully for the future of Guatemala, he was arrested and has been in jail for seven years now. False evidence was used to put him there. This is completely unfair, as he has done nothing wrong. You must do what is right and release him from prison immediately.

Yours sincerely, ¹⁰

Elena

What is the purpose of the letter?

① to demand that Manuel should be freed from prison

② to explain that the land near the Cahabón river is dying

③ to apologize for Manuel's behavior and ask for forgiveness

④ to suggest a possible way to protect the Guatemalan culture

⑤ to ask for the construction of the power plants to be slowed down

Summary / Graphic Organizer

A Choose the correct words to fill in the blanks.

| organizes | released | protect | governments | arrested | prisoners |

Reading 1

Every year from December 10 to 17, Amnesty International _____ Write for Rights. The purpose of this event is to write letters and free innocent prisoners around the world. Each year, thousands of letters are sent to _____ that have innocent people in jail. And many _____ have been released because of these letters. To take part in the event, download the information pack from the Amnesty International homepage. Then get together with friends or classmates and write letters! It's a great way to _____ human rights.

Reading 2

The writer insists that Manuel Morales should be _____ because he fought peacefully to protect the Cahabón river area and was put in jail unfairly.

Vocabulary

B Complete each sentence with the best word.

| organize | apologize | innocent | construction | pack | hero | protect |

1 You should _____ to her because you made a mistake.

2 The building is still under _____.

3 She insisted that she was _____ and did nothing wrong.

4 You should wear your helmet to _____ yourself.

5 My friends helped to _____ the party.

6 He is the _____ who saved the child from the car accident.

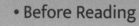

Reading 1

Pretzels are delicious treats made of wheat flour dough. Some of them are soft like bread, and others are hard like cookies. You can recognize pretzels by their shape, which is twisted like a knot. Although pretzels originally came from Europe, they are now one of America's most popular snacks. You can find them for sale at bakeries, movie theaters, and sports events. 5

Pretzels were invented in the seventh century in Southern France. Some monks were baking bread one day. One of the monks decided to make his bread in the shape 10 of a child's arms folded to pray. This monk gave some of the special bread to children for being good and praying. (ⓐ) Thus, these twisted snacks were nicknamed *pretiola*, the Latin word for "little reward." (ⓑ) Pretiolas soon became popular throughout Europe, and their name changed to "pretzels." (ⓒ) Later, pretzels traveled to America on the boats of the early settlers. (ⓓ) 15

Today, people eat pretzels for breakfast in Austria. In Germany and Switzerland, people cut pretzels open and put butter on them. In America, you can try pretzels of many different _____(A)_____ ! Soft pretzel varieties include sweet cinnamon, sesame, garlic butter, 20 and honey mustard. Some hard pretzels are covered in yogurt or chocolate. <u>Whether you like them sweet, salty, soft, or hard, pretzels certainly are a delicious "little reward"!</u>

1 **What is the passage mainly about?**

① the recipe for pretzels

② the history of pretzels

③ the inventors of different pretzels

④ the advantages of eating pretzels

2 **What shape were the first pretzels made to look like?**

_____

3 **Where would the following sentence best fit?**

> It was in Pennsylvania that the first pretzel bakery in the United
> States was opened.

① ⓐ   ② ⓑ   ③ ⓒ   ④ ⓓ

4 **What is the best choice for blank (A)?**

① prices

② colors

③ flavors

④ shapes

5 **What does the underlined sentence mean?**

① Pretzels are not only delicious but also healthy.

② All kinds of pretzels are delicious and enjoyable.

③ People should take the chance to try various pretzels.

④ Pretzels are very useful to give as a reward to children.

6 **Write T if the statement is true and F if it's false.**

(1) Pretzels are twisted so that they taste better.

(2) People in Germany and Switzerland eat pretzels with butter.

Hard pretzels were invented by mistake in Pennsylvania, USA, in the late 1700s. One day, a baker's helper fell asleep while baking pretzels over a fire.

(A) Not only were the hard pretzels tasty, but they could be stored longer because they were dry. Hard pretzels are now just as popular as soft ones! 5

(B) However, while throwing the pretzels out, he tasted one. The overcooked pretzel was hard, crunchy, and delicious! The master baker was surprised.

(C) As a result, he baked the pretzels for twice as long as usual. When the master baker came back and saw what had happened, he shouted at his helper. 10

Choose the best order of (A), (B), and (C) after the given text.

① (A) – (C) – (B)

② (B) – (A) – (C)

③ (B) – (C) – (A)

④ (C) – (A) – (B)

⑤ (C) – (B) – (A)

Summary / Graphic Organizer

A Choose the correct words to fill in the blanks.

mistake   settlers   reward   varieties   praying   spreads

Reading 1

Pretzels —— It's a popular snack in a special shape.

A monk bakes bread in the shape of a _____ child's arms.

▼

Eventually known as a "pretzel," it _____ through Europe.

▼

The pretzel is brought to America by early _____.

▼

Many different _____ and flavors are created.

Reading 2

Thanks to a helper's _____ in baking pretzels for too long, we can enjoy hard pretzels today.

Vocabulary

B Choose the correct word for each definition.

settler   shout   crunchy   recognize   dough   twist   reward

1 to bend or turn something into a different shape: _____

2 someone who moves to a new place where few people live: _____

3 something that you receive after you have done something good: _____

4 a mix of flour and water for baking: _____

5 firm and making a loud noise when you eat it: _____

6 to speak in a loud voice, especially in order to be heard more easily: _____

UNIT 04 Jobs

Reading 1

Many jobs that were common in the past do not exist anymore. Some have disappeared because of lifestyle changes, while others have become unnecessary due to advancing technology. Let's look at a few examples.

In the 1600s, some people worked 5 as herb strewers. Rich families hired them to spread herbs and flowers around their house. At that time, proper soap was expensive, and houses didn't have plumbing or hot water. 10 This made it difficult for people to bathe often. So the herbs and flowers were used to hide their bad smell! Nowadays, most people have access to hot water and soap, so herb strewers no longer exist.

Cutting ice is another job that is no longer necessary. Before fridges, ice was difficult to get. So ice cutters would use a 15 horse-powered device to cut blocks of ice from frozen lakes. This job was quite difficult because they had to face extreme weather conditions. _____(A)_____ modern fridges were invented, however, ice cutters haven't been needed anymore.

Lastly, companies no longer require professional typists. 20 Before computers were invented, companies needed to hire a lot of typists to type their documents. But today, computers have made this job completely unnecessary. In fact, computers can even produce documents by recording speech!

As the world changes and technologies advance, more jobs will become 25 unnecessary. Which jobs do you think will disappear next?

1 **What is the passage mainly about?**

① popular jobs in recent years

② some unsuccessful jobs in the past

③ jobs that used to exist but no longer do

④ why some jobs cannot be replaced by computers

2 **What is mentioned as a reason that some jobs disappeared? (Choose two.)**

① increased population

② improved human rights

③ changes in our way of life

④ the development of modern technology

3 **Why did rich families hire herb strewers?**

① to learn how to use herbs

② to grow rare species of herbs

③ to decorate their gardens with herbs

④ to cover their bad smell by spreading herbs

4 **What is the best choice for blank (A)?**

① Since

② Though

③ As long as

④ Otherwise

5 **What is NOT true about ice cutters?**

① They used a device pulled by horses.

② They cut ice from the frozen ground in winter.

③ Because of the extremely cold weather, their work was hard.

④ They became unnecessary after fridges were invented.

6 **These days, computers can even create documents by _____**

_____ .

Will robots take all our jobs in the future? The answer is no. This is because many jobs require human qualities. For example, only humans can be writers. Writing is a form of art, and writers produce content from their own experiences, ideas, and imagination. It is a difficult task, and robots lack the ability to do it. Robots can't do the job of a lawyer either. Being a lawyer involves 5 a lot of analysis and negotiation. They need to understand complicated laws and argue the cases of their clients. Robots are not capable of these types of things. Since many jobs can only be done by a real human with a heart and a brain, robots will never fully replace us in the workforce. 10

To summarize the passage, what is the best choice for blanks (A) and (B)?

Human workers cannot be completely _____(A)_____ by robots because many jobs _____(B)_____ workers with human qualities.

	(A)		(B)
①	used	—	need
②	produced	—	lack
③	replaced	—	require
④	involved	—	take
⑤	switched	—	provide

Summary / Graphic Organizer

A   Choose the correct words to fill in the blanks.

| spreading | typed | lifestyle | frozen | access | computer |

Reading 1

Jobs That Disappeared

Herb Strewers	• covered bad smells by _____ herbs and flowers around the house → easy _____ to hot water and soap
Ice Cutters	• cut blocks of ice from _____ lakes → the invention of the fridge
Typists	• _____ documents for companies → the invention of the _____

Vocabulary

B   Complete each sentence with the best word.

| imagination | hire | case | professional | face | negotiation | disappear |

1   Children are usually full of _____.

2   The contract is under _____.

3   They watched the man _____ into the smoke.

4   The company is going to _____ a new employee.

5   They have to _____ their problems instead of running from them.

6   They are _____ musicians, not amateurs.

UNIT 05 Animals

• Before Reading   Do you know what kind of food gorillas enjoy?

Reading 1

As the sun rises over Bwindi National Park in Uganda, a family of gorillas is waking up. They come out of their leafy beds, sit down a few meters away, and start eating the nearby plants. While the gorillas are eating, a scientist is observing what kinds of plants they eat. Why? Because ⁵ gorillas naturally choose foods that may also be healthy for humans!

Research into gorillas' eating habits began in the 1980s. Back then, scientists realized that chimpanzees always eat a particular plant when ⓐ they have a stomachache. ¹⁰ It was later discovered that this plant can cure stomachaches in humans by killing germs. Some scientists decided to study the diet of animals in order to find more plants which act as medicines. ⓑ They chose gorillas because gorillas eat so many different kinds of plants; thus the possibility of discovering useful medicines goes up. In the forest, the scientists collect samples of gorillas' favorite foods. Then ¹⁵ ⓒ they test them to find out their various uses.

So far, the scientists have found 71 different kinds of plants that gorillas like to eat. ⓓ They think at least three of these plants may be medicines. It will take some time to test all the different plants. But thanks to gorillas, people may someday benefit from these medicines. ²⁰

24

1   **What is the best title for the passage?**

① A Gorilla Family's Typical Day

② When You Feel Sick, Ask a Gorilla

③ What's the Best Food for Gorillas?

④ Make Your Own Natural Medicine!

2   **Scientists began their research into gorillas' eating habits because they found that _____.**

① gorillas' bodies are very much like humans'

② chimpanzees and gorillas always eat healthy plants

③ chimpanzees eat a plant that can also cure humans

④ chimpanzees and gorillas live much longer than other animals

3   **Why did the scientists choose to study gorillas?**

_____, so the

scientists are more likely to discover useful medicines.

4   **According to the passage, what is NOT something scientists do in their research?**

① watch carefully what gorillas eat

② give gorillas some plants to eat

③ get samples of gorillas' favorite plants

④ check the medical effects of some plants

5   **Which is NOT referring to the same thing?**

① ⓐ   ② ⓑ   ③ ⓒ   ④ ⓓ

6   **Which of the following best describes these medicines in the 3rd paragraph?**

① wild and natural

② simple and clean

③ old and powerful

④ special and expensive

Gorillas are just like humans in many ways. They have two legs and arms, ten fingers and toes, and even 32 teeth like us. They spend their days caring for one another, eating, playing, and sleeping together. Sadly, these beautiful and intelligent creatures are seriously endangered. There are now very few gorillas left, and they face many threats. The biggest problem   5
is that they are losing their homes. People cut down their forests for wood. Also, hunters try to kill gorillas and make money from selling their meat. We must make an effort to protect these "gentle giants." Otherwise, they will soon   10
disappear, and we may not see their friendly faces again.

To summarize the passage, what is the best choice for blanks (A) and (B)?

Because gorillas deal with many _____(A)_____ against their homes and lives, they are critically ____(B)____ .

	(A)		(B)
①	attacks	—	friendly
②	activities	—	intelligent
③	changes	—	sold
④	threats	—	endangered
⑤	problems	—	protected

Summary / Graphic Organizer

A Choose the correct words to fill in the blanks.

samples	eat	medicines	humans	observe

Reading 1

In the 1980s, scientists saw chimpanzees eating a plant to cure their stomachaches. They realized that the same plant also cured stomachaches in _____. Because of this, they started a project to study what animals _____. They chose gorillas because they eat such a wide variety of plants. The scientists follow the gorillas and take _____ of the plants they eat. Then they test them to see if they can be used as _____ for humans. So far three plants are thought to be a cure for illness.

Vocabulary

B Choose the correct word for each definition.

friendly	discover	threat	medicine	germ	creature	intelligent

1 to find something for the first time: _____

2 any living thing that is not a plant: _____

3 able to think, understand, and learn things: _____

4 something given to sick people to make them well: _____

5 a tiny living thing that can cause disease: _____

6 a person, thing, or a situation that may be harmful or dangerous: _____

• **Before Reading**   Who is your favorite baseball player?

Reading 1

"If you have an opportunity to make things better and you don't, you are wasting your time on this earth."

These are the words of Roberto Clemente, the first Hispanic baseball player to become a star in the Major Leagues. He was born in Puerto Rico and joined the Major Leagues in 1955. At first, he had a hard time because he didn't speak English well. But eventually he became one of the sport's best players, winning the World Series twice. He was also named the league's MVP in 1966.

However, Clemente is even better remembered for caring about others. He helped poor people and fought to change some bad ideas about Hispanics and African-Americans. When a terrible earthquake hit Nicaragua in 1972, Clemente decided to go there himself and help. But sadly, his plane, which was carrying the aid packages, crashed into the ocean. He was only 37 and his body was never found.

After his death, Clemente was added to the Baseball Hall of Fame. In Puerto Rico, a sports camp for children was created in his honor. And every year, the Major Leaguer who does the most to help others is given the Roberto Clemente Award. Clemente was truly someone who

_____ (A) _____ .

1 **What is the best title for the passage?**

① More Than Just a Baseball Player

② Baseball Players in the Hall of Fame

③ Historic Moments in American Baseball

④ The Life of Hispanic Baseball Players in America

2 **Clemente had a hard time when he joined the Major Leagues because** _____.

3 **Which word best describes the 3rd paragraph?**

① hopeful   ② tragic

③ pleasant   ④ adventurous

4 **What is NOT mentioned as something people did after Clemente died?**

① put him in the Baseball Hall of Fame

② built a sports camp in Puerto Rico for kids

③ continued helping people after the earthquake in Nicaragua

④ created an award named after him

5 **What is the best choice for blank (A)?**

① made the world a better place

② showed that dreaming is important

③ loved baseball more than anyone else

④ saved many people's lives in Latin America

6 **What is NOT mentioned about Clemente in the passage?**

① where he was born

② how he helped people

③ how he died

④ why he became a baseball player

Before Roberto Clemente, there was another great baseball player who _____. In 1946, Jackie Robinson became the first African-American Major League Baseball player. Before that time, African-Americans had to play in a different league. So, when he first started playing in the Major Leagues, some fans and other players yelled terrible things ⁵ at him. But Robinson didn't give up. He soon won everyone's respect with his terrific play. He was even chosen as the league's MVP in 1947. Before long, there were many other African-Americans in the Major Leagues. This was an important step toward making America a great place to live for people of any color. ¹⁰

What is the best choice for the blank?

① helped people in need

② changed American society

③ overcame physical difficulties

④ started a special baseball league

⑤ made baseball popular in America

Summary / Graphic Organizer

A Choose the correct words to fill in the blanks.

packages	award	Hispanic	earthquake	won

Reading 1 The Life of Roberto Clemente

A player	– was the first _____ Major League star – _____ the World Series twice and was the Major League MVP in 1966
A helper	– helped Hispanics and African-Americans, as well as poor people – died while trying to help _____ victims
After his death	– He was added to the Baseball Hall of Fame. – A sports camp for children was built in Puerto Rico. – A special _____ was named after him.

Vocabulary

B Complete each sentence with the best word.

eventually	moment	give up	named	respect	aid	join

1 He is trustworthy and has earned the _____ of everyone.

2 To get better at soccer, why not _____ a soccer club?

3 Congratulations! You've been _____ the player of the year.

4 After talking with each other for a long time, they _____ agreed.

5 Right after the war, the country was very poor. It received _____ from many countries.

6 Despite all the difficulties, she refused to _____ and achieved her dream.

Reading 1

The Third Day in Poland

Today was the third day of our vacation in Poland. We headed for the Wieliczka Salt Mine. That's right! It is a salt mine, not a gold mine. Anyway, the Wieliczka mine is a famous tourist attraction because deep inside it are statues, galleries, and churches—all made of salt! It is over 600 5 years old. Our guide told us that millions of years ago, there was a sea there. How interesting!

We walked down more than 350 steps to enter the mine. (ⓐ) The air underground was cool and damp. (ⓑ) They looked just like real people! (ⓒ) I also saw beautiful paintings on the wall. (ⓓ) 10 Some of the caves were churches—yes, salt churches! So who made all of these? The miners did! In the nineteenth century, miners spent nearly all day underground. They wanted a place to pray, so they built churches inside the mine. Nowadays there are 3.5 km of tunnels filled with beautiful salt attractions. With floors, ceilings, walls, and even chandeliers made of salt, I felt like I was in a dream world. 15

At the end of our tour, we were 327 meters underground. I think that was the deepest place I have ever been in my life. To leave the mine, we took an elevator up. The sunlight was too bright for my eyes, but I was glad to see it again.

1 What is the passage mainly about?

① the secrets of salt mining

② brave salt miners in Poland

③ Wieliczka's beautiful salt mine

④ the importance of salt in the 19th century

2 According to the passage, why do many tourists visit the Wieliczka Salt Mine?

① because it is the oldest mine in the world

② because everything inside it is made of salt

③ because they can see miners working there

④ because there is a guide who tells interesting stories

3 Where would the following sentence best fit?

As we walked through the tunnels, I saw statues of Polish kings and queens.

① ⓐ   ② ⓑ   ③ ⓒ   ④ ⓓ

4 The miners built churches inside the mine because _____ _____.

5 Which of the following best describes how the writer feels in the 2nd paragraph?

① proud

② scared

③ amazed

④ exhausted

6 What is NOT something the writer did in the mine?

① The writer walked deep underground.

② The writer passed by beautiful salt attractions.

③ The writer met a few miners in the salt church.

④ The writer took an elevator to leave the mine.

Today, we can buy salt cheaply at the store. A long time ago, however, it was thought to be very valuable. Salt not only makes food taste better and keeps our bodies healthy, but it also helps preserve food. Therefore, salt was much more important at that time than it is today. However, not all 5 parts of the world had enough salt. In these places, salt was such a valuable item that sometimes it was even used as _____. Actually, in ancient Rome, soldiers' payment was salt. This was known as *salarium*, and that's where the word "salary" comes from.

What is the best choice for the blank?

① fuel

② money

③ cleaner

④ medicine

⑤ seasoning

Unit Review

Summary / Graphic Organizer

A Choose the correct words to fill in the blanks.

miners steps sea valuable salt attraction

Reading 1

The Wieliczka Salt Mine in Poland is a popular tourist _____. It is more than 600 years old. A long time ago, the mine was actually a(n) _____. Now its underground tunnels are a place for tourists to visit. An amazing fact about the mine is that all the things inside it are made of _____. There are statues, galleries, and even churches in it. It is said that _____ built the churches so they could have a place to pray.

Reading 2

Unlike today, salt was incredibly _____ in the past because of its many benefits and limited amount.

Vocabulary

B Choose the correct word for each definition.

pray valuable preserve mine ceiling head for gallery

1 to move toward something: _____

2 to keep food fresh for a very long time: _____

3 to speak to a god to give thanks or ask for help: _____

4 a deep place where people get minerals such as coal and gold: _____

5 very important, helpful, or useful: _____

6 the inner surface on the top of a room: _____

• Before Reading   Have you ever been to a ballpark to watch a game?

Reading 1

Many factors can influence the result of a baseball game. But did you know that the baseball park itself has an important effect on how the game is played? Most sports are played on fields that are all exactly the same, but not baseball. While all ballparks must follow the same ⁵ measurements for the infield, the outfield is different in each one. That means each playing field can be different in size and shape. _____(A)_____, some fields have fences that are higher or lower than others. And some have roofs, but others don't. ¹⁰

Because of these differences, there are ballparks where teams are more likely to score a lot of runs, and parks that usually see low-scoring games. The first group are known as "hitter's parks," while those in the second group are "pitcher's parks." The Astros' <u>Minute Maid Park</u> in Houston, Texas is a hitter's park. Its outfield is rather small, so a hit that would be an easy out at another park is often a home run ¹⁵ at Minute Maid. Both coaches and players know these differences, and they'll often change strategies according to which park they play in.

The _____(B)_____ of baseball parks is something that makes the sport more exciting. Each park, like each game, is different. Therefore, fans never know what's going to happen. ²⁰

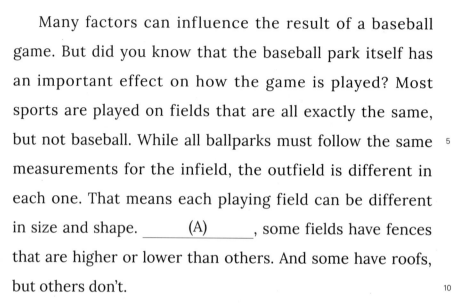

1 **What is the best title for the passage?**

① No Two Ballparks Are Alike

② The Most Popular Baseball Park

③ Successful Strategies for Baseball

④ Baseball: America's Favorite Sport

2 **What is the best choice for blank (A)?**

① However

② Moreover

③ In contrast

④ Nonetheless

3 **Why does the writer mention <u>Minute Maid Park</u>?**

① to show the importance of hitters

② to give an example of a hitter's park

③ to say how many home runs were hit at hitter's parks

④ to explain why hitter's parks are more common than pitcher's parks

4 **Home runs are common at Minute Maid Park because** _____

_____ .

5 **What is the best choice for blank (B)?**

① challenge

② advantage

③ importance

④ uniqueness

6 **Which of the following is NOT true about baseball parks?**

① All baseball parks have the same size infield.

② There are no fences or roofs at hitter's parks.

③ At pitcher's parks, teams don't often score many runs.

④ Where a game is played can affect what strategy is used.

You've probably seen baseball fields many times. But there are some places that might not be so familiar: the dugouts and the bullpens. A dugout is an area on the side of the field. There is a bench inside it for players to sit on during the game. ⓐ There are also places for players to keep their equipment, such as ⁵ helmets and bats. ⓑ It's common for them to get all of their equipment for free from sports companies. ⓒ On one side of the dugout, there is usually a place called a bullpen. ⓓ This is where pitchers can warm up before entering a game. ⓔ Just like the field, a bullpen has a pitcher's mound and a home plate.

Which sentence is NOT needed in the passage?

① ⓐ   ② ⓑ   ③ ⓒ   ④ ⓓ   ⑤ ⓔ

Summary / Graphic Organizer

A Choose the correct words to fill in the blanks.

pitcher's	warm up	catch	hitter's	strategies	infield

Reading 1

Cause	All ballparks are different except for the size of the _____.

▼

Effect	1. At a(n) _____ park, it's easier to hit home runs. At a(n) _____ park, teams don't score many runs. 2. Coaches and players change their _____ according to the park.

Reading 2

In baseball, each team has a dugout where they can sit and a bullpen where the pitchers can _____ for the game.

Vocabulary

B Complete each sentence with the best word.

score	area	fence	influence	factor	according to	strategy

1 Exercise is an important _____ in keeping your body healthy.

2 Do not enter. This _____ is for employees only.

3 Thankfully, everything went _____ plan.

4 She's made a decision already, so your advice won't _____ her.

5 He built a(n) _____ around the yard to keep his family safe.

6 We need to develop a(n) _____ for dealing with air pollution.

Technology

Reading 1

AI, or artificial intelligence, is a word for systems or machines that are programmed to perform tasks and improve themselves with information. Nowadays, AI is not only bringing rapid changes to technological fields, but also playing an important role in the art world. 5

For example, take a look at Ludwig van Beethoven's unfinished symphony, which remained incomplete since 1827. In addition to all of Beethoven's works and notes, AI was given the works of musicians who influenced him. As if it were human, the AI studied them and was able to identify 10 patterns and style choices in Beethoven's work. After, it put all of the information together and completed the work.

Another example can be found in the discovery of a(n) _____(A)_____ Pablo Picasso painting. With the help of high-tech cameras, scientists found *The Lonesome Crouching Nude* beneath *The Blind Man's Meal*. As the painting was painted over, 15 they had to use X-rays to see it. Then came the hard part: recreating the painting. The outline was recovered through image processing and AI was trained to paint the image like Picasso did. After 118 years of being covered, the painting was brought to life through 3D printing.

20   Thanks to AI, we can enjoy amazing artwork _____(B)_____ . The use of AI technology in the field of art will surely expand its possibilities.

Technology

1　**What is the passage mainly about?**

① ways to find imaginary artwork

② why an incomplete symphony exists

③ the popularity of AI in the field of music

④ the meaningful role of AI to the art world

2　**What is the best choice for blank (A)?**

① hidden

② forbidden

③ destroyed

④ exposed

3　**After identifying** _____ **, AI**

put all of the data together and finished Beethoven's symphony.

4　**What can be inferred from the underlined sentence?**

① Picasso's painting looked livelier as a 3D painting.

② Picasso's painting was revealed using 3D printing.

③ Picasso's painting was sold at an unbelievably high price.

④ Picasso's painting became animated through 3D painting.

5　**What is the best choice for blank (B)?**

① found completely finished

② created by unknown artists

③ that could have been lost in history

④ that may have been damaged by machines

6　**Write T if the statement is true and F if it's false.**

(1) To complete Beethoven's unfinished symphony, Beethoven and other musicians' works were entered into the AI.

(2) High-tech cameras and X-rays were used to find and see *The Blind Man's Meal*.

What can I help you with?

We always hear about how Artificial Intelligence (AI) is constantly evolving and getting better and better. But, how is AI actually being added to our everyday lives? Well, AI has the ability to figure out the best way to achieve a specific goal. It does this through deep learning, in which the AI studies and grows ⁵ its knowledge in select areas. Because of this, AI can be changed to meet our needs. Businesses can use AI chatbots to answer any customer questions online by translating a customer's words. On the other hand, hospitals can use AI doctors to detect, diagnose, and treat illness by collecting and observing a patient's data. In the future, we may see the day when AI even takes over ¹⁰ annoying everyday tasks!

What is the best title for the passage?

① AI in Our Everyday Lives

② Categorizing: What Makes AI Great

③ Our Future without AI: A Total Disaster

④ Jobs That AI Can Do Better than Humans

⑤ How AI and Deep Learning Were Invented

Summary / Graphic Organizer

A Choose the correct words to fill in the blanks.

beneath	studied	recreate	related	unfinished

Reading 1

Artificial Intelligence in Artwork

Beethoven's Symphony
- One of Beethoven's symphonies remained _____ since 1827.
- AI studied the works of Beethoven and other musicians _____ to him.
- → AI identified the patterns and style choices of Beethoven and completed his work.

Picasso's Painting
- One of Pablo Picasso's paintings was hidden _____ another painting.
- To find and _____ his painting, high-tech cameras, X-rays, and a 3D printer were used.
- → AI was trained to paint in Picasso's style and recreated the work.

Vocabulary

B Choose the correct word for each definition.

recover	role	popularity	achieve	select	rapid	illness

1 the purpose or position that a person or thing has: _____

2 chosen over others for certain reasons: _____

3 the state of being well liked by many people: _____

4 happening suddenly or quickly in a short amount of time: _____

5 to successfully complete something or reach a particular goal: _____

6 a disease that affects the mind or the body: _____

Reading 1

Dear Dr. Kay,

I have a problem at school. Before a test, my hands sweat and my heart beats fast. Then during the test, I get nervous and change my answers many times. So I usually get a low score. What can I do?   5

Chris

Feeling nervous about tests is normal. Just ask any student! But many people get too nervous, and their stress can stop them from doing well. Here are some ways to reduce test anxiety.

First, remember that _____(A)_____. Stress is your body's sign that   10
something important is going to happen. So take an active approach. Let stress remind you to study well for each test. And remember, the body and brain use stress to perform better. Second, watch out for negative thoughts. ⓐ Negative thoughts can increase stress, so replace them with positive ones. ⓑ Changing answers often doesn't help a lot. ⓒ Try to think things like "I'm going to do my best!" and "I've   15
studied hard, so I can pass!" ⓓ This will help you relax and do your best. Third, learn from past mistakes. If last time you didn't study the right material or gave the wrong answers, try to learn from that experience. Knowing how to turn _____(B)_____ into _____(C)_____ is a valuable skill! Finally, take care of your health. Studies show   20
that getting enough sleep, exercising, and eating healthy food can release stress, which can improve test performance.

Dr. Kay

1   **What is the Chris's problem?**

① He cannot sleep because of test anxiety.

② He cannot decide on a plan for his future.

③ He experiences a lot of stress when taking tests.

④ He becomes nervous when he meets new people.

2   **What is the best choice for blank (A)?**

① you must get rid of stress

② a little stress can help you

③ stress is not good for your health

④ feeling nervous has nothing to do with stress

3   **Which sentence is NOT needed in the passage?**

① ⓐ   ② ⓑ   ③ ⓒ   ④ ⓓ

4   **What is NOT suggested about test anxiety?**

① It is more serious with teenagers.

② It is experienced by many people.

③ It can be used to improve your score.

④ It can be controlled by your way of thinking.

5   **What is the best pair for blanks (B) and (C)?**

① bad luck   —   useful tools

② sad memories   —   good dreams

③ past failures   —   future successes

④ difficult questions   —   correct answers

6   **What is Chris UNLIKELY to do to reduce his test anxiety if he follows the advice?**

① try to relax by being more positive

② stay up all night to prepare for tests

③ review the mistakes he made after each test

④ work out three times a week to keep his body healthy

Do you ever feel extreme stress over studying? The Pomodoro technique can help you stay focused through the use of time management. The technique came from a man who used a timer shaped like a tomato—or, *pomodoro* in Italian— to study. You can use it to manage time and improve concentration. First, 5 divide large goals into small, 25-minute tasks. Once you finish a task, take a short break, which represents the end of one pomodoro. After completing four pomodoros, take a longer break so you can process the information. Use this technique to get work done without feeling overly anxious. You can always change the number of pomodoros to complete. With each goal 10 _____, you'll be shocked by how much you can do!

What is the best choice for the blank?

① planned with enough time

② managed in a different way

③ set with necessary information

④ broken down into smaller parts

⑤ shared with as many people as possible

Summary / Graphic Organizer

A Choose the correct words to fill in the blanks.

| manage   help   normal   health   nervous   mistakes   positive |

Reading 1

Problem	getting _____ before and during tests → poor test scores
Solutions	1. Use stress to _____ you study hard. 2. Think only _____ thoughts. 3. Learn from your past _____. 4. Make sure you take care of your _____.

Reading 2

With the Pomodoro technique, you can _____ your time by dividing tasks into smaller parts and taking breaks between each one.

Vocabulary

B Complete each sentence with the best word.

| approach   divide   relax   beating   performance   get rid of   active |

1 The man is alive—his heart is still slowly _____.

2 We need to _____ these vegetables. They've gone bad.

3 To become a leader, you need to develop a(n) _____ personality.

4 I've already tried that. We need a more creative _____ to the problem.

5 This was the actor's best _____ of his entire career.

6 Listen to soft music to _____ your body and mind.

The Environment

Reading 1

Climate change is probably the world's biggest problem. (ⓐ) Many people already know this. (ⓑ) "Climate refugees" are being created in different parts of the world. (ⓒ) These are people who have lost their homelands because of climate change. (ⓓ)   5

Actually, most of these problems are caused by the pollution from developed countries. <u>Poor countries aren't responsible for the climate change that's affecting our world.</u> But sadly, almost all climate refugees come from poor countries. This includes countries like Tuvalu in the   10 Pacific Ocean. Because of climate change, the sea level around Tuvalu has risen 1.2 millimeters per year for the past 23 years. Scientists are worried that by the end of the 21st century, Tuvalu could sink into the sea. In addition to rising seas, climate change produces dangerous storms. Many people in Bangladesh have moved to India as climate refugees to escape the storms.   15

Climate refugees face many problems. Away from home, they have no place to live and no jobs. In addition, they are not welcomed by many countries. Some countries are trying to help the refugees and working to stop climate change. But this is not enough. The whole world needs to work together to solve this problem.

1 What is the best title for the passage?

① Moving to the Sea
② War Refugees in Danger
③ Surviving Natural Disasters
④ Climate Refugees in Trouble

2 Where would the following sentence best fit?

But most people don't know that climate change is already harming people's lives.

① ⓐ   ② ⓑ   ③ ⓒ   ④ ⓓ

3 What does the underlined sentence mean?

① Climate change makes poor countries much poorer.
② Poor countries do not think climate change is a big problem.
③ It is believed that climate change is caused by poor countries.
④ Pollution from poor countries doesn't greatly affect climate change.

4 According to the scientists, what could happen to Tuvalu by the end of the 21st century?

_____

5 What is the best pair for blanks (A) and (B)?

The writer thinks the world should ____(A)____ climate change and ____(B)____ climate refugees.

	(A)	(B)
①	learn to stop	— give up on
②	be ready for	— build homes for
③	keep developing	— take care of
④	take responsibility for	— work to help

6 Write T if the statement is true and F if it's false.

(1) Most climate refugees come from poor countries.
(2) Many Indian people went to Bangladesh to escape the storms.

A Call to Save the Future of Tuvalu

On November 5th, 2021, Tuvaluan minister Simon Kofe urged the United Nations to quickly act against climate change. His goal was to raise awareness about the effects of rising sea levels on the island nation. As always, Kofe wore a suit and tie when delivering his speech. But instead of on land, he stood knee-deep in water. Like many other parts of the island, the area used to be land. "Climate change won't wait for us," he said.

Low-lying islands like Tuvalu are sinking into the ocean, which worries the people. The minister pleaded for his islands, saying, "They were the home of our ancestors, they are the home of our people today, and we want them to remain the home of our people into the future." Tuvaluans fear that they may have to leave their homes if nothing changes.

5

10

15

What does the underlined sentence mean?

① Climate change issues have remained unsolved.

② It's too late to realize how serious climate change is.

③ We have to take immediate action on climate change.

④ We should take some time to prepare for climate change.

⑤ People on the island no longer worry about rising sea levels.

Summary / Graphic Organizer

A Choose the correct words to fill in the blanks.

poor	developed	homelands	responsible	storms	sink

Reading 1

Our planet's changing climate is causing many problems. People who must leave their _____ because of climate change are known as "climate refugees." Most of these people come from _____ countries. The island of Tuvalu might sink into the ocean, for example, and Bangladesh is having terrible _____. However, it is pollution from _____ countries that is the main cause of climate change. These countries should help climate refugees and work to stop climate change.

Reading 2

Tuvaluan minister Simon Kofe urged the United Nations to act quickly against climate change because it is causing low-lying islands to _____ into the ocean.

Vocabulary

B Choose the correct word for each definition.

escape	refugee	urge	ancestor	solve	climate	affect

1 to get away from something bad: _____

2 to find an answer to a problem: _____

3 someone who is forced to leave his or her country: _____

4 a family member who lived many years ago: _____

5 the typical weather patterns of a particular place: _____

6 to persuade or strongly advise someone to do something: _____

• Before Reading   Could you survive on an island all on your own?

Reading 1

Robinson Crusoe was a British sailor. During a trip, a storm destroyed his ship, and he was left on an island. He thought he was the only one living there, but...

The *cannibals were busy preparing for their dinner party. They weren't looking at their prisoner. I watched him secretly untie his ropes. Then he suddenly jumped up and started running quickly toward the stream. Three of the cannibals chased him, shouting angrily. I wanted to help him, so I jumped out from behind the rock. I shot my gun straight into the air — BANG! The cannibals were so frightened by the noise of my gun that they ran away.

The poor prisoner stood nearby. He was cold, wet, and very frightened. I didn't know his name, so I called him Friday. That day was Friday, and I couldn't think of a better name. I spoke gently to him and smiled a lot. Although he didn't understand my language, he could see that I was friendly. He came closer and began to move his hands up and down. I could tell that he was thanking me for saving his life.

I led him up the hill to my home. I invited him to sit down and gave him some food— bread and cheese. When was the last time that I had shared a meal with someone else? Surely it had been more than twenty years! When he finished eating, Friday fell fast asleep on the floor.

*cannibal: a person who eats human flesh

5

10

15

20

1   **What is the best title for the passage?**

① Robinson Crusoe Hunts Animals

② Robinson Crusoe Kills an Enemy

③ Robinson Crusoe Makes a Friend

④ Robinson Crusoe Fights the Pirates

2   **What did Crusoe do to help the prisoner escape?**

_____

3   **Why did Crusoe call the prisoner "Friday"?**

① because Friday was his best friend's name

② because the prisoner was born on a Friday

③ because Friday was his favorite day of the week

④ because it was Friday when he saved the prisoner

4   **How do Friday's feelings change throughout the story?**

① sad → proud

② bored → excited

③ afraid → relieved

④ frightened → disappointed

5   **What is NOT suggested in the passage?**

① The cannibals had caught Friday and tied him up.

② Friday doesn't trust Crusoe.

③ Friday can't understand what Crusoe says.

④ Crusoe has been alone for a long time.

6   **Write T if the statement is true and F if it's false.**

(1) Friday tried to run away while the cannibals were fighting with each other.

(2) Crusoe was kind to Friday and gave him food.

Robinson Crusoe is a novel written by an English writer, Daniel Defoe, in 1719. It is a very famous novel, and it has been popular with readers for almost 300 years. However, few people know that the story of Robinson Crusoe _____. In 1704, Daniel Defoe heard about a ⁵ Scottish sailor called Alexander Selkirk. He had a fight with his ship's captain and was left on a small island near Chile. He stayed alone there for four years before he was rescued. After hearing about Selkirk's experience, Defoe wrote *Robinson Crusoe*. Interestingly, in 1966 the name of the island was changed to "Robinson Crusoe Island" in honor of the much-loved character. ¹⁰

What is the best choice for the blank?

① inspired other famous novels

② came from an old Scottish legend

③ was actually based on a true story

④ was first written by an unknown author

⑤ was from Defoe's experience as a sailor

Summary / Graphic Organizer

A Choose the correct words to fill in the blanks.

gun	share	escaped	friendly	alone	chased

Reading 1

Robinson Crusoe watched as some cannibals prepared to eat a prisoner. But then the prisoner _____ from his ropes and began to run. Crusoe jumped out from his hiding place and shot his _____ into the sky. The loud noise caused the cannibals to run away. Crusoe smiled to show the man that he was _____. He decided to call the man Friday. Crusoe took Friday home and fed him, glad to _____ a meal with someone after so many years. Shortly after, Friday fell asleep.

Reading 2

Daniel Defoe wrote *Robinson Crusoe* after hearing about a Scottish sailor who was _____ on an island for four years.

Vocabulary

B Complete each sentence with the best word.

destroyed	chasing	novel	share	is based on	untie	in honor of

1 There is only one chocolate bar, so let's _____ it.

2 The policeman was _____ the thief down the street.

3 You should _____ the ribbon first to open the box.

4 The US renamed the airport _____ President Kennedy.

5 The story of this film is not imaginary. It _____ real events.

6 A lot of houses were _____ by the earthquake.

Reading 1

What color is the number 4? Is the month of May sad or happy? To most people, these questions are nonsense. But to those who have a special sense known as synesthesia, they aren't crazy at all. Synesthesia affects the way people sense and think about things. It is the mixing of one sense, ⁵ such as sight, with another one, such as hearing.

There are more than 60 different types of synesthesia that have been reported. For example, some people automatically think of a color when they see a certain letter or number. Others may hear a certain sound every time ¹⁰ they smell a rose. There have been many famous people with synesthesia. One of them was the Russian painter Wassily Kandinsky. He experienced the mixed senses of _____(A)_____. As he painted, he heard the music that was made by each color.

(ⓐ) Despite the fact that we know a lot about synesthesia, scientists still don't know exactly what causes it. (ⓑ) They think there is some confusion in the brain. ¹⁵ (ⓒ) Parts of the brain that are supposed to belong to one sense are used by another. (ⓓ) In fact, some scientists think that a large number of children have synesthesia. As they grow older, the strange connections in their brains disappear.

1 **What is the best title for the passage?**

① Ways to Be a Creative Thinker

② When Two Different Senses Meet

③ The Importance of Brain-Based Education

④ Famous Artists and Their Unique Diseases

2 **A question like "What color is the number 4?" doesn't sound strange to those _____.**

3 **What is the best choice for blank (A)?**

① smell and hearing   ② sight and hearing

③ smell and touch   ④ sight and taste

4 **Where would the following sentence best fit?**

> These "connections" between different areas of the brain are probably created at birth.

① ⓐ   ② ⓑ   ③ ⓒ   ④ ⓓ

5 **What is NOT true according to the passage?**

① More than 60 kinds of synesthesia have been discovered so far.

② Artists experience synesthesia more often than normal people.

③ Synesthesia is thought to be caused by confusion between different parts of the brain.

④ A little boy with synesthesia may lose his mixed senses as he grows up.

6 **According to the passage, who does NOT seem to have synesthesia?**

① Tom: I hear a sad melody when I look at this painting.

② Julie: I can find the number 2 very quickly because it's always blue.

③ Bob: I smell flowers whenever I listen to the violin part in this song.

④ Kate: I can memorize long words while listening to loud music.

You might hear synesthesia mentioned in a poetry class. That's because the term "synesthesia" is used when a poet expresses a connection between the senses. For example, a poet may talk about "a hard, metallic sound" or "a delicious feeling." (ⓐ) In fact, synesthesia is common in English. (ⓑ) Synesthesia is also talked about in music, because people tend to connect musical tones with particular colors. (ⓒ) While real synesthesia is not very common, people seem to be able to easily understand it. (ⓓ) So, try to imagine "a silky voice" or "a dark red sound." (ⓔ) You should find it easy.

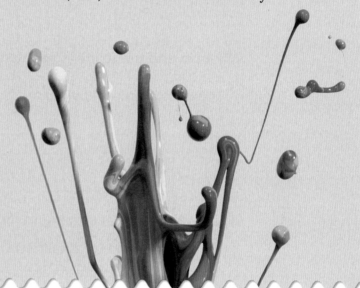

Where would the following sentence best fit?

> In general, people connect high tones with light colors and low tones with dark ones.

① ⓐ   ② ⓑ   ③ ⓒ   ④ ⓓ   ⑤ ⓔ

Summary / Graphic Organizer

A Choose the correct words to fill in the blanks.

birth	mixed	types	connection	nonsense	wrong

Reading 1

Synesthesia

- a condition in which a person's senses get _____ together
- more than 60 _____

Example
- a certain letter or number → a color
- the smell of a rose → a certain sound

Possible Cause
- A person's senses seem to use the _____ parts of the brain.
- This confusion may begin at _____.

Reading 2

Synesthesia is often used in English and in music to make a _____ between different senses.

Vocabulary

B Choose the correct word for each definition.

sense	term	metallic	silky	mention	sight	confusion

1 the ability to see: _____

2 a situation in which things are not clear: _____

3 having a smooth, soft, and shiny look or feel: _____

4 to briefly talk or write about someone or something: _____

5 a word or phrase that has a specific meaning: _____

6 the ability of seeing, hearing, smelling, tasting, or feeling: _____

The Economy

• Before Reading   What do you consider most when choosing a product?

Reading 1

Shopping can be difficult. There are just too many products to choose from! So marketers use special techniques to make customers choose their products. One of these is known as the "hunger marketing strategy."

First, an attractive, new product is introduced. Next, ⁵ the company only sells a small amount of the product. This makes it seem like there isn't enough for everyone, since demand for the product is much higher than the supply. Later, the company sells the product in large amounts and makes a big profit. Hunger marketing also helps the ¹⁰ company's brand image. When many people want something they cannot easily get, their opinion of the product _____(A)_____.

ⓐ Apple is one company that uses this technique successfully. ⓑ Every time they create a new product, there are long lines of people waiting to buy it. ⓒ Apple's first product was the Apple Computer 1. ⓓ That's because the company ¹⁵ carefully controls the supply and keeps it low. _____(B)_____, Apple can continue to have a popular brand image. Xiaomi, a Chinese smartphone manufacturer, uses hunger marketing in a slightly different way. Not only do they make their products hard to get, but they also set their prices very low.

So next time you're waiting in line to buy ²⁰ a new product, ask yourself this question: Is this product really hard to get, or is this just another example of hunger marketing?

1 **What is the best title for the passage?**

① Attractive Designs, Big Profits

② A "Hard to Get" Marketing Strategy

③ A Popular Marketing Technique of the Past

④ Big Competition Between High-Tech Companies

2 **Why do some companies only sell a small amount of their products at first?**

① because there are not enough products to sell

② because the products aren't popular with customers

③ because the companies want to increase the demand

④ because other companies sell small amounts of the same product

3 **What is the best choice for blank (A)?**

① goes up

② goes down

③ does not change

④ becomes unknown

4 **Which sentence is NOT needed in the passage?**

① ⓐ   ② ⓑ   ③ ⓒ   ④ ⓓ

5 **What is the best choice for blank (B)?**

① However

② Otherwise

③ As a result

④ For example

6 **Write T if the statement is true and F if it's false.**

(1) Hunger marketing isn't profitable, since only small amounts of the product are sold.

(2) Xiaomi raises the cost of its products when using hunger marketing.

FOMO

> Let's say you visit an online shop for fun, and suddenly an advertisement appears that says "You just missed it! Our newest keyboard sold out yesterday."

(A) Don't let them fool you. Always focusing on what others have and what you are lacking can be incredibly stressful. Rather than focusing on what you are missing in life, try focusing on what you really need. Then you can spend more wisely.

(B) Thinking you've missed an opportunity, you buy another keyboard to avoid losing out on a deal again. Congratulations—you just fell for FOMO marketing.

(C) FOMO is the "fear of missing out" on what others have. You can feel like others are living better lives when they have something you don't. So by using this technique, marketers lead customers into making thoughtless and unnecessary purchases.

Choose the best order of (A), (B), and (C) after the given text.

① (A) – (C) – (B)

② (B) – (A) – (C)

③ (B) – (C) – (A)

④ (C) – (A) – (B)

⑤ (C) – (B) – (A)

Summary / Graphic Organizer

A Choose the correct words to fill in the blanks.

supply large introduced missing out demand small

Reading 1   **How Hunger Marketing Works**

A new product is _____ .

▼

The company sells the product only in _____ amounts.

▼

The _____ for the product increases.

▼

The company sells the product in _____ numbers and makes a profit.

Reading 2

Customers make unnecessary purchases because of their "fear of _____"
on things.

Vocabulary

B Complete each sentence with the best word.

appear control opinion slightly purchase focus on fool

1 Please give us your _____ on the matter during the meeting.

2 The government must do more to _____ the spread of the virus.

3 You have to compare prices before you make a(n) _____ .

4 I could not _____ the exam because of the noise.

5 Famous actors often _____ on TV shows or films.

6 The clown tried to _____ me, but I wasn't tricked.

Reading 1

Jack has a few energy bars every day for his health. Sally eats energy bars to lose weight. They're making a healthy choice, aren't they? Some people might think so, but Jack and Sally should know that _____(A)_____.

Commercials tell us that these bars give us more energy 5 and can even help us think better. Because of this, many people feel that they are a kind of health food. However, most energy bars are actually full of sugar, caffeine, or fat. Therefore, eating too many of them can be harmful to your health. This is especially true for people who eat more than 10 two bars a day or eat them instead of a regular meal. While energy bars may be more nutritious than chips, candy, and other junk foods, they are not as healthy as a full meal.

Energy bars also contain a large number of calories. ⓐMany bars are produced with a high calorie count to give energy to athletes. ⓑSome high calorie foods 15 provide energy but are not tasty. ⓒHowever, when ordinary people eat these bars regularly, they receive too many calories. ⓓThis can lead to weight gain and other health problems.

An occasional energy bar can help people who need to have a fast meal or prepare for physical activity. 20 But eating too many can be more harmful than eating none at all.

1   **What is the passage mainly about?**

   ① the truth about energy bars

   ② various types of energy bars

   ③ the benefits of eating energy bars

   ④ reasons why people eat energy bars

2   **What is the best choice for blank (A)?**

   ① energy bars make them feel healthy

   ② energy bars can be a good source of energy

   ③ energy bars do not have any nutritious value

   ④ energy bars may not be as good as they think

3   **Commercials say that energy bars** _____

_____.

4   **Which sentence is NOT needed in the passage?**

   ① ⓐ   ② ⓑ   ③ ⓒ   ④ ⓓ

5   **What is NOT true about energy bars?**

   ① They may be high in sugar, caffeine, or fat.

   ② They are healthier than chips or candy.

   ③ They are as good as a regular meal.

   ④ They have lots of calories.

6   **Which of the following best describes energy bars?**

   ① No news is good news.

   ② Good medicine tastes bitter.

   ③ Too much is worse than too little.

   ④ Nothing ventured, nothing gained.

Understanding the Nutrition Facts Label:
A Can of Vegetable Soup

Nutrition facts labels help people understand what's in the food they eat. Here is a nutrition facts label for a can of vegetable soup. "Serving Size" shows the amount of the product normally eaten in one meal. ⓐ On this label, one serving of soup equals one cup, which is 230 g. "Servings Per Container" shows how many servings there are in this can. ⓑ If you eat the whole can of this soup, you eat two servings. ⓒ That doubles the calories and nutrients on the label. "Calories" shows the calories per serving, not for the whole container. So, if you want to buy a low-calorie product, be sure to check both the calories and the serving size. ⓓ For this soup, the whole container has two cups, and the calories for all of it is 80. "% Daily Value" shows how much of key nutrients are contained in each serving based on a daily diet of 2,000 calories. If one serving has less than 5% for a certain nutrient, this is considered a little. And if there is more than 20%, this is a lot. ⓔ According to the label, this soup has too much sodium.

5

10

15

Nutrition Facts		
Serving Size 1 cup (230g)		
Servings Per Container 2		
Amount Per Serving		
Calories 80		
		% Daily Value
Total Fat 0.5g		1%
Saturated Fat 0g		0%
Trans Fat 0g		0%
Cholesterol 0g		0%
Sodium 960mg		40%
Total Carbohydrate 17g		6%
Dietary Fiber 2g		
Sugars 4g		
Protein less than 4g		
Vitamin A 10%	Vitamin C 0%	
Calcium 4%	Iron 4%	

Which sentence is NOT true about the nutrition facts label above?

① ⓐ   ② ⓑ   ③ ⓒ   ④ ⓓ   ⑤ ⓔ

Summary / Graphic Organizer

A Choose the correct words to fill in the blanks.

calories	weight	harmful	commercials	regular	fast

Reading 1

Energy Bars

Problems	- _____ say they give us energy and help us think better. - Many people think they are a kind of health food.
Facts	- They are full of sugar, caffeine, or fat. - Eating too many of them can be _____ to your health. - They are not as healthy as a _____ meal. - They contain a lot of _____.
Advice	- Eat them occasionally when you need to eat _____ or prepare for physical activity.

Vocabulary

B Choose the correct word for each definition.

athlete	daily	occasional	commercial	activity	serving	physical

1 a thing that you spend time doing: _____

2 a person who participates in sports: _____

3 done or happening every day: _____

4 happening sometimes, but not often: _____

5 relating to a person's body and not their mind: _____

6 an amount of one type of food that is enough for one person: _____

Reading 1

The Henley-on-Todd Regatta is a "boat" race held every year on the Todd River in Alice Springs, Australia. This boat race is unique because the Todd River is actually a dried-up river that usually has no water in it.

It was started in 1962 by a local man who wanted to   5
raise money for charity. (ⓐ) He got his idea from the famous Henley-on-Thames Regatta. (ⓑ) As he had hoped, the boat race, held in the hot, deep sand of the Todd River, was very entertaining. (ⓒ) Over the years, the Henley-on-Todd Regatta became a day of celebration and   10
silly races. (ⓓ)

In the main race, teams must run through hot, dry sand. Because the "boats" have no bottoms, the teams have to hold them while they are running! Everyone laughs and cheers as the teams try to reach the finish line. Afterwards, there are canoe races in which sand shovels are used instead of oars. The final event is the   15
popular battleship contest. Trucks decorated as battleships race along the sand, and their teams fight with flour bombs and water cannons!

Being highly entertaining, the race draws large crowds every year. Best of all, since it began, it has raised over a million dollars for various charities around the world.

1   **What is the best title for the passage?**

① Silly Races Around the World

② Visit the Amazing Todd River!

③ The Driest Boat Race on Earth

④ Enjoy the Fastest Boat in the World!

2   **The Todd River is a strange place for a boat race because**

_____ .

3   **Where would the following sentence best fit?**

It is a boat race held each year in England.

① ⓐ   ② ⓑ   ③ ⓒ   ④ ⓓ

4   **What is NOT mentioned about the Henley-on-Todd Regatta?**

① when it was first held

② why it was invented

③ when you can sign up for it

④ where the idea came from

5   **What is NOT true about the Henley-on-Todd Regatta races?**

① People carry the "boats" while they are running.

② People move canoes forward with sand shovels.

③ Teams fight in a battleship contest using flour and water.

④ The team that makes the crowd laugh the most wins the race.

6   **What is the best pair for blanks (A) and (B)?**

The Henley-on-Todd Regatta is an event that both ___(A)___ and ___(B)___ people.

	(A)		(B)
①	teaches	—	encourages
②	helps	—	entertains
③	strengthens	—	excites
④	challenges	—	surprises

The Henley-on-Thames Regatta is a rowing race held every July on the River Thames in England. It was first held in 1839 and lasted for just one day. It now lasts for five days and includes rowing teams from around the world. The event is so popular that teams must compete beforehand to win a place in the competition. On each day of the regatta, there are up to 100 races with ⁵ just two boats competing in each race. <u>However, the boat races are just half the attraction!</u> The regatta is also famous for attracting rich and important people, including the British Royal Family. Thus, many people visit the event hoping to see a prince or princess in the crowd!

What does the underlined sentence mean?

① There is also something else to enjoy.

② Only half of the races are very popular.

③ The boat races don't attract many people.

④ The boat races are not as interesting as before.

⑤ Half of the rowing teams can compete in each race.

Summary / Graphic Organizer

A Choose the correct words to fill in the blanks.

crowds bottomless dried-up fun rowing charity shovels

Reading 1

Every year, the town of Alice Springs in Australia holds the Henley-on-Todd Regatta. It is a boat race on a _____ river. It was started in 1962 to raise money for _____. Teams race through the sand, holding up their _____ boats as they run. There are also canoe races using _____ instead of oars. The final event is the battleship contest. Trucks decorated like battleships race as their passengers fight with water and flour. It's a very _____ event, and it raises lots of money for charity.

Reading 2

At the Henley-on-Thames Regatta, people can watch _____ teams race in a competition, and they might even see the British Royal Family.

Vocabulary

B Complete each sentence with the best word.

decorated raised charity main cheered competition up to

1 The crowd _____ loudly when the home team scored a goal.

2 All the money we have _____ at the event will be given to the poor.

3 We _____ the room with flowers and candles for the party.

4 The stadium in my town can hold _____ 100,000 people.

5 The _____ difference between these two products is their design.

6 There is intense _____ between athletes to win a gold medal.

Reading 1

If you're like most teenagers, then you probably use various social networking services. These services let you create a profile, post information about yourself, and communicate with your friends. They are great fun. However, if you aren't careful when using them, they can ⁵ cause trouble in your real life.

When using social networking services, you have to remember that whatever you post online will always be there. Even if you delete it, it's easy for others to copy, save, and send it. Moreover, you never know who is looking ¹⁰ at your information. Once you put it online, it becomes _____(A)_____. Posting inappropriate material can also create problems for you. In fact, you can even get arrested for posting inappropriate content online.

To make sure this doesn't happen to you, there are some steps you can take. First, if you can make your online profile private, you should. This will allow you to ¹⁵ decide who can see your information. Second, use good online etiquette. Don't say or post harmful things online. A good rule is this: If you wouldn't do something in real life, don't do it online! Finally, you should never agree to meet online friends in real life if you don't already know them. Your "friend" could actually be someone who wants to hurt you.

1 **What is the best title for the passage?**

① Protect Yourself Online

② Use Your Computer Wisely

③ Changes in Social Networking Services

④ How to Make Your Blog Fun and Useful

2 **What is the best choice for blank (A)?**

① true

② public

③ negative

④ important

3 **According to the passage, who is LEAST likely to have trouble?**

① Jessica: My online profile can only be viewed by me.

② Patrick: I share my online photos with anyone who visits my page.

③ Christy: I like to post rumors about others to attract visitors to my page.

④ Chase: I enjoy meeting new people who I get to know online.

4 **What is NOT mentioned in the passage?**

① what people usually do on social networking services

② how social networking services became popular

③ the characteristics of social networking services

④ ways to avoid trouble on social networking services

5 **What is the writer's attitude toward the topic?**

① proud

② upset

③ cautious

④ surprised

6 **Write T if the statement is true and F if it's false.**

(1) The information on social networking services quickly disappears.

(2) What you do wrong online can affect you offline.

> With the growing popularity of the internet, cyberbullying is becoming a serious problem.

(A) Moreover, cyberbullying messages spread quickly to a very wide audience. To stop cyberbullying, parents and teachers should understand how serious it is. And if you're being bullied, the first thing to do is to tell someone. You must speak out and find help. 5

(B) This is because bullying in cyberspace is much easier, as it's difficult to find out who the bully is. Also, online bullies can reach their victims anytime and anyplace, even at home.

(C) Cyberbullying is any kind of online bullying, such as sending threatening 10 messages or stealing another person's password. It can be more harmful than other acts of bullying.

Choose the best order of (A), (B), and (C) after the given text.

① (A) – (C) – (B)

② (B) – (A) – (C)

③ (B) – (C) – (A)

④ (C) – (A) – (B)

⑤ (C) – (B) – (A)

Summary / Graphic Organizer

A Choose the correct words to fill in the blanks.

private	save	victims	communicate	manners	remove

Reading 1 — **Using Social Networking Services**

Why	- They are a good way to _____ with friends. - They are a lot of fun.
Problems	- Posted information is difficult to _____. - You don't know who is reading your personal information.
Advice	- Keep your online profile _____. - Use good _____ when posting online. - Don't agree to meet online friends in real life.

Reading 2

Cyberbullying is a serious problem because bullies can easily use the internet to greatly harm their _____.

Vocabulary

B Choose the correct word for each definition.

post	rumor	private	etiquette	threatening	various	delete

1 different and more than a few: _____

2 to put something onto a website: _____

3 a set of rules about how to behave: _____

4 information or a story that may be true or false: _____

5 to cross out or remove something that was written: _____

6 only used by or available to a particular person or group of people: _____

• **Before Reading** Have you ever seen the musical *Wicked*?
What was it about?

Reading 1

If you've only seen Elphaba, the Wicked Witch of the
West, in the movie *The Wizard of Oz*, then you probably
think that she's a really mean character. But once you watch
the musical *Wicked*, you'll be surprised to know that she is
actually a good witch!   5

The musical is based on Gregory Maguire's novel.
Maguire wanted people to hear Elphaba's side of the story.
ⓐ The writer of the musical was inspired by his novel but
decided not to follow it exactly. ⓑ Instead, she focused on
the untold stories of Elphaba and her unlikely friendship   10
with Glinda. ⓒ Because of the musical's moving storylines and memorable songs,
Wicked has won many major awards and continues to enjoy success worldwide.
ⓓ Tony Awards are given to outstanding Broadway plays each year.

The musical follows Elphaba from birth to college and through many
life-changing events. And the viewers see how she is always judged unfairly because   15
of her green skin. But over the course of the story, they learn that Elphaba is a
good person. She stands up for
others and does her best to fight
injustice in the land of Oz.

_____(A)_____, the viewers   20
learn that Glinda the Good and
the Wizard of Oz are not as kind
or as wise as they seem. As they
find out more about Oz's secrets,
they realize that there are always   25
two sides to every story.

1 **What is the best title for the passage?**

① Wicked: The Wonder of Magic

② Wicked: Elphaba's Side of the Story

③ Elphaba and Glinda: The Heroes of Oz

④ Elphaba: The Most Famous Witch in the World

2 **Which sentence is NOT needed in the passage?**

① ⓐ   ② ⓑ   ③ ⓒ   ④ ⓓ

3 **What is NOT true about the musical *Wicked*?**

① Its story is exactly the same as Gregory Maguire's novel.

② It has won many awards due to its impressive storylines and songs.

③ It's still popular around the world.

④ It tells Elphaba's life story.

4 **The writer says Elphaba is actually a good person because she**

_____

_____ .

5 **What is the best choice for blank (A)?**

① Otherwise

② For instance

③ In other words

④ On the other hand

6 **According to the passage, what can you learn from Elphaba and Glinda's story?**

① There's no place like home.

② The early bird gets the worm.

③ Don't judge a book by its cover.

④ Birds of a feather flock together.

Frequently Asked Questions about *Wicked*

Question 1   **How long has *Wicked* been running?**

The first performance of *Wicked* was on October 30, 2003 in New York City. As of April 24, 2022, its 7,082 performances make it the fifth-longest running show on Broadway! The show lasts for about two and a half hours with a fifteen-minute break.

5

Question 2   **What is the show like?**

Wicked has beautiful Tony Award-winning sets and costumes, and impressive songs that will transport you to the magical world of Oz in no time!

Question 3   **Will kids like *Wicked*?**

Kids who like *The Wizard of Oz* also enjoy watching *Wicked*! But before buying tickets for younger children, parents should take the show's running time into consideration. Also, the show's flying monkeys may scare some children. But, in general, kids aged eight and up will find *Wicked* delightful.

10

What is NOT true about the musical *Wicked*?

① It was first performed in 2003 in New York.

② It takes about two hours with a half-hour break.

③ Its sets and costumes were recognized with Tony Awards.

④ There is a scene of monkeys flying.

⑤ It is enjoyable for kids aged eight and above.

Summary / Graphic Organizer

A Choose the correct words to fill in the blanks.

good	unfairly	fights	judges	novel	sides

Reading 1

Wicked is a famous musical based on Gregory Maguire's _____. It tells the story of Elphaba, the Wicked Witch of the West from *The Wizard of Oz*. In the musical, however, Elphaba is revealed as being a(n) _____ witch. She is treated _____, but she stands up for others and _____ injustice. Viewers also learn that Glinda the Good and the Wizard of Oz are not as kind as they seem. Through memorable songs and storylines, viewers learn that there are always two _____ to every story.

Vocabulary

B Complete each sentence with the best word.

break	mean	realize	memorable	run	injustice	character

1 Today's lecture will focus on _____ in our society.

2 The novel's main _____ was based on the author's mother.

3 Global wars often make us _____ the importance of peace.

4 Chris always takes a(n) _____ before doing his homework.

5 Kate wants to have a(n) _____ experience this summer vacation.

6 You should not be so _____ to your friends.

Reading 1

On April 12, 1961, the Soviets became the first country to put a human in space. From the deserts of Kazakhstan, a spacecraft called *Vostok 1* was launched towards the stars. The flight lasted 108 minutes, long enough to make one circle around Earth. *Vostok 1* reached as high as 200 miles 5 above Earth.

Vostok's pilot had to record everything he observed. But he didn't have control of the craft during the flight. This was because no one knew how a person would be affected out in space. For example, low gravity in space might have 10 caused the pilot to pass out. So the craft was controlled from the ground.

So who was the lucky person who got to become the "_____(A)_____"? It was Yuri Gagarin, a major in the Soviet Air Force. It is said that he was selected partly because of his size. He was only a little more than five feet tall. This made it easy for him to fit and move around in *Vostok 1*. Also, his friendly and easygoing 15 character helped him go through the hard training for the historic flight.

The success of *Vostok 1* encouraged more space programs, showing that humans could survive space travel. Soon, many more astronauts joined Gagarin on the list of people who had traveled to space.

1 **What is the passage mainly about?**

① Soviet space programs

② people who traveled in space

③ the first manned space journey

④ the development of space travel

2 **According to the passage, why did people on Earth control the spacecraft?**

① because they were better trained than Gagarin

② because some astronauts passed out on other flights

③ because Gagarin had to record what he saw in space

④ because they were not sure what would happen to Gagarin

3 **What is the best choice for blank (A)?**

① Last Man in Space

② Father of the Moon

③ Messenger of Hope

④ Columbus of the Cosmos

4 Gagarin's short height was an advantage because it _____

_____.

5 **What does the underlined sentence mean?**

① Many other people succeeded in traveling to space.

② Other astronauts were more successful than Gagarin.

③ Gagarin met many astronauts while traveling in space.

④ There was a list of people who wanted to travel to space.

6 **What is NOT mentioned in the passage?**

① where the craft was sent from

② how long the flight lasted

③ Gagarin's feelings during the flight

④ the result of Gagarin's flight

Have you ever wondered what space smells like? If you asked a group of astronauts, they might say it smells like walnuts, burnt steak, or burning metal. (ⓐ) They experience these strange smells whenever they take their helmets off after a spacewalk. (ⓑ) Scientists are still not certain about what causes this mix of smells, but they have some theories. (ⓒ) One theory suggests that the smells come from dying stars. (ⓓ) These chemicals drift around the universe and take part in the creation of other stars and planets. (ⓔ) They can also be found on Earth and are often created when we burn oil, coal, or even food.

5

Where would the following sentence best fit?

When stars die, they release a mixture of smelly chemicals into space.

① ⓐ ② ⓑ ③ ⓒ ④ ⓓ ⑤ ⓔ

Summary / Graphic Organizer

A Choose the correct words to fill in the blanks.

launched	smell	size	human	gravity	controlled

Reading 1

The first _____ went to space on April 12, 1961. His name was Yuri Gagarin, and he traveled in a Soviet spacecraft called *Vostok 1*. It was _____ from the Kazakhstan desert and flew 200 miles above Earth. Since no one knew what effect space would have on Gagarin, the craft was _____ from the ground. One reason Gagarin was chosen for the historic flight was his small _____, which allowed him to move around the spacecraft easily. Afterwards, many others followed the brave astronaut into space.

Reading 2

Some scientists believe that space's strange _____ comes from the chemicals released by dying stars.

Vocabulary

B Choose the correct word for each definition.

record	astronaut	easygoing	select	planet	theory	wonder

1 being relaxed and not easily angered: _____

2 someone who travels to and works in space: _____

3 to write down some information to keep it for the future: _____

4 to think about something because you are curious about it: _____

5 a possible explanation for how or why something happens: _____

6 a large round object that travels around a star: _____

Reading 1

During the Hundred Years' War, the English army captured the French city of Calais. The king of England promised not to harm its people if six leaders, or *burghers, surrendered to be killed. Six leaders agreed to give up their lives right away. Through this action, the city was saved, and the king decided not to kill the brave men.

More than 500 years later, in 1880, the government of Calais wanted to honor the burghers by building a statue. They hired Auguste Rodin, the most famous sculptor of the time, for the project. He worked on the statue for the next ten years. When he finally finished, however, the city leaders were not very pleased. *The Burghers of Calais* was not like any other statue. Instead of looking proud and heroic, the six men in the statue seemed tired and worried. It was because Rodin wanted to show their _____(A)_____. He thought they probably had felt proud, but had been afraid of their coming death at the same time. Also, the statue was not on top of a high base as most heroic statues were. It was at the same height as the people who looked at it.

Although there was much debate over Rodin's work, it remained in Calais. Today, it is considered a masterpiece and an important example of changing styles in sculpture. Rodin's effort to show the inner side of the burghers is still inspiring many artists today.

*burgher: a respected citizen of a town

1 **What is the passage mainly about?**

① Rodin's new style of statue

② Rodin's unhappy life in Calais

③ the popularity of Rodin's sculptures

④ the changing style of Rodin's works

2 **Which of the following best describes the story of the six burghers?**

① tragic

② touching

③ humorous

④ mysterious

3 **The government of Calais had the statue made because they**

_____.

4 **What is the best choice for blank (A)?**

① brave actions

② true emotions

③ great popularity

④ historical meaning

5 **What can be inferred from the 2nd paragraph?**

① Many people in Calais helped Rodin finish the statue quickly.

② Rodin didn't have an interest in making *The Burghers of Calais*.

③ The city leaders expected their heroes to look courageous in the statue.

④ People were prevented from seeing *The Burghers of Calais* by the city leaders.

6 **Write T if the statement is true and F if it's false.**

(1) *The Burghers of Calais* was not liked by some people at first.

(2) Rodin wanted to put his statue above the people who look at it.

Auguste Rodin was born in Paris in 1840. He became interested in art at an early age, but his career as a sculptor was not _____. He was not accepted to art school and had to work to support his family by doing decorative stonework. Finally, after a long time, people began to realize how talented he was. ⁵ His great works include *The Gates of Hell*, *The Thinker*, and *The Burghers of Calais*. His sculptures are known for their strength and realism. They show both the passion and the weakness of people. Today, Rodin is considered one of the greatest sculptors of his time.

What is the best choice for the blank?

① over

② easy

③ lonely

④ special

⑤ successful

Unit Review

Summary / Graphic Organizer

A Choose the correct words to fill in the blanks.

| afraid   government   statue   challenges   great   heroes |

Reading 1

The Burghers of Calais

— a(n) _____ created by Auguste Rodin

— showed six _____ from the Hundred Years' War

— controversial, as it showed the men as tired and _____

— now considered to be a(n) _____ work of art

Reading 2

Though Auguste Rodin faced many _____ in his career, he is now thought to be among the best sculptors of his time.

Vocabulary

B Complete each sentence with the best word.

| sculptures   passion   debate   talented   surrender   honor   heroic |

1 The country made a new holiday to _____ the brave soldiers.

2 I saw some modern _____ at the museum.

3 Jenny is a great student. Her _____ for learning is amazing.

4 The firefighters made a(n) _____ effort to save the people.

5 The students held a(n) _____ about gun control.

6 He waved the white flag to _____ to the enemy.

Photo credits

JUNIOR
READING EXPERT

A Theme-Based Reading Course for Young EFL Learners

Level 4

Word Book

Origins

commonly	(부) 보통, 흔히
fairly	(부) 꽤, 상당히
origin	(명) 기원
mystery	(명) 수수께끼, 미스터리
come from	유래하다
reveal	(동) 드러내다, 밝히다
language	(명) 언어
scholar	(명) 학자
discover	(동) 발견하다
editor	(명) 편집자
make fun of	~을 놀리다
spelling	(명) 철자법, 맞춤법
joke	(동) 놀리다, 농담하다 (명) 농담
incorrect	(형) 부정확한
correct	(형) 정확한 (동) 바로잡다, 정정하다
run for	~에 입후보하다
reelection	(명) 재선
president	(명) 대통령
nickname	(명) 별명
campaign	(명) 캠페인, 선거 운동
supporter	(명) 지지자
support	(동) 지지하다

shorten	통 짧게 하다
chant	통 구호를 외치다
vote	통 투표하다
rally	명 집회, 대회
politician	명 정치인, 정치가
history	명 역사
originate	통 비롯되다, 유래하다
reason	명 이유
spell	통 철자를 쓰다
common	형 흔한
phrase	명 구절
communicate	통 의사소통하다
communication	명 의사소통
distance	명 거리
likely	부 아마도
technology	명 기술
advance	통 증진되다, 진전을 보이다
original	형 원래의
necessary	형 필요한
influence	명 영향

international	형 국제적인, 국제의
human right	인권
take part in	~에 참가하다
free	형 자유로운 동 석방하다
innocent	형 순결한; 무고한
prisoner	명 죄수, 포로
organize	동 조직하다, 개최하다
organization	명 단체, 조직
amnesty	명 사면
government	명 정부
jail	명 감옥
lawyer	명 변호사
journalist	명 보도 기자, 언론인
put in jail	감옥에 보내다
speak out	거리낌 없이 말하다, 의견을 말하다
take notice of	~을 알아차리다
hold	동 잡다; 개최하다
pack	명 꾸러미, 팩
protect	동 보호하다
defend	동 지키다, 옹호하다
accuse	동 고발[기소/비난]하다
hero	명 영웅

surrounding	혱 인근의, 주변의
construction	몡 건설
power plant	발전소
area	몡 지역
destruction	몡 파괴
peacefully	붱 평화롭게
future	몡 미래
arrest	동 체포하다
false	혱 잘못된, 거짓의
evidence	몡 증거
completely	붱 완전히
unfair	혱 불공평한
release	동 석방하다
prison	몡 감옥
immediately	붱 즉시
demand	동 요구하다
apologize	동 사과하다
behavior	몡 행동
forgiveness	몡 용서
slow down	늦추다

treat	몡 만족[즐거움]을 주는 것
wheat flour	밀가루
dough	몡 반죽
recognize	동 알아보다
twist	동 꼬다, 감다
knot	몡 매듭
originally	부 원래, 처음에는
for sale	팔려고 내놓은
monk	몡 수도사, 승려
fold	동 접다, 구부리다
pray	동 기도하다
reward	몡 보상, 사례
settler	몡 이주자, 정착민
variety	몡 다양(성); 종류
cinnamon	몡 계피
sesame	몡 참깨
cover	동 덮다, 바르다
certainly	부 확실히
advantage	몡 이점, 이익
flavor	몡 맛, 풍미
by mistake	실수로
late	형 늦은; 후반의

helper	몡 도와주는 사람, 조수
tasty	혱 맛있는
taste	동 맛보다
store	동 저장하다
throw out	내던지다, 버리다
overcooked	혱 지나치게[너무] 구워진
crunchy	혱 바삭바삭한
master	몡 주인
shout	동 소리를 지르다

UNIT 04 Jobs

exist	동 존재하다
disappear	동 사라지다
lifestyle	몡 생활 방식
unnecessary	혱 불필요한
due to	~ 때문에
herb strewer	약초 뿌리는 사람
hire	동 고용하다
spread	동 뿌리다, 흩뿌리다
proper	혱 적절한, 제대로 된
plumbing	몡 배관
bathe	동 목욕하다

hide	통 숨기다
have access to	~에 접근할 수 있다
no longer	더 이상 ~않은
fridge	명 냉장고
horse-powered	형 마력의
device	명 장치
face	통 직면하다
extreme	형 극도의, 극심한
invent	통 발명하다
require	통 필요로 하다, 요구하다
professional	형 전문적인
document	명 문서
replace	통 대체하다
population	명 인구
development	명 발전
rare species	희귀종
decorate	통 장식하다, 꾸미다
quality	명 자질
content	명 내용
imagination	명 상상(력)
lack	통 부족하다
ability	명 능력
involve	통 수반[포함]하다, 필요로 하다
analysis	명 분석

negotiation	명 협상
complicated	형 복잡한
law	명 법
argue	동 논의하다
case	명 사건
client	명 고객
be capable of	~할 수 있다
workforce	명 노동력, 노동 인구
switch	동 바꾸다

UNIT 05 Animals

leafy	형 잎이 우거진; 잎으로 된
nearby	형 근처의
observe	동 관찰하다
naturally	부 천성적으로
particular	형 특정한
stomachache	명 배탈, 복통
discover	동 발견하다
cure	동 치료하다
germ	명 세균
diet	명 식습관, (일상의) 음식물
medicine	명 약

thus	(부) 그러므로, 따라서
collect	(동) 모으다
various	(형) 다양한
so far	지금까지
at least	적어도
benefit from	~의 혜택을 누리다
typical	(형) 전형적인
medical	(형) 의학적인
effect	(명) 효과
care for	~을 돌보다
intelligent	(형) 지능이 있는, 영리한
creature	(동) 생물
seriously	(부) 심각하게
endangered	(형) 멸종 위기에 처한
threat	(명) 위협
lose	(동) 잃다
make an effort	노력하다
friendly	(형) 친근한, 정다운
deal with	다루다, 대하다
critically	(부) 위태롭게

People

opportunity	몡 기회
Hispanic	혱 라틴 아메리카계의 몡 라틴 아메리카계의 사람
join	동 가입하다, 합류하다
eventually	뷩 결국
twice	뷩 두 번
name	동 명명하다; 지명하다
MVP	(스포츠) 최우수 선수 (most valuable player)
care about	~에 관심을 가지다
African-American	몡 아프리카계 미국인 혱 아프리카계 미국인의
earthquake	몡 지진
aid	몡 원조, 도움
package	몡 꾸러미, 소포
crash	동 추락하다, 충돌하다
body	몡 몸; 시신
Hall of Fame	명예의 전당
in one's honor	~을 기념하여
award	몡 상
truly	뷩 진정으로
historic	혱 역사적으로 중요한
moment	몡 순간
tragic	혱 비극적인
adventurous	혱 모험적인

continue	통 계속하다
be named after	~의 이름을 따서 이름 지어지다
save	통 저장하다; 구하다
yell	통 외쳐 말하다
give up	포기하다
respect	명 존경, 존중
terrific	형 멋진
before long	머지않아
toward	전 ~을 향하여
in need	어려움에 처한
overcome	통 극복하다
physical	형 신체의
difficulty	명 어려움, 곤경

UNIT 07 Places

head for	~로 향하다
mine	명 광산 통 캐다, 채굴하다
miner	명 광부
tourist attraction	관광 명소
attraction	명 볼거리, 매력
statue	명 조각상
gallery	명 미술관

church	몡 교회
step	몡 걸음; 계단
underground	뿐 지하에
damp	혱 습기 찬, 축축한
cave	몡 동굴
nearly	뿐 거의
pray	뙝 기도하다
nowadays	뿐 오늘날에는
be filled with	~로 가득 차다
ceiling	몡 천장
chandelier	몡 샹들리에
scared	혱 겁에 질린
exhausted	혱 지친
cheaply	뿐 저렴하게
valuable	혱 귀중한
preserve	뙝 보존하다, 보관하다
item	몡 품목
ancient	혱 고대의
soldier	몡 군인
payment	몡 지불; 보수
be known as	~라고 알려지다
salary	몡 월급, 급료
fuel	몡 연료
cleaner	몡 세제

seasoning	몡 양념

UNIT 08 *Sports*

factor	몡 요인, 요소
influence	몡 영향 통 ~에 영향을 주다
result	몡 결과
have an effect on	~에 영향을 미치다
field	몡 들판; 경기장
exactly	뷔 정확하게
ballpark	몡 야구장
measurement	몡 측량; 치수
infield	몡 내야
outfield	몡 외야
fence	몡 담장
score	통 득점하다, 얻다
run	통 득점
hitter	몡 타자
hit	몡 안타
pitcher	몡 투수
strategy	몡 전략
according to	~에 따라
alike	혱 서로 닮은, 비슷한

in contrast	대조적으로
challenge	몡 도전
advantage	몡 이익, 강점
uniqueness	몡 독특함[성]
familiar	혱 친숙한
dugout	몡 더그아웃
bullpen	몡 불펜
area	몡 지역, 장소
side	몡 측면, 옆 부분
equipment	몡 장비, 기기
common	혱 공통의; 흔한
warm up	준비운동을 하다
mound	몡 흙무더기; (투수의) 마운드
home plate	홈플레이트

UNIT 09 Technology

artificial intelligence	인공 지능(AI)
program	동 프로그램을 짜다[설정하다]
perform	동 수행하다
improve	동 향상시키다
rapid	혱 빠른
field	몡 분야

play a role	역할을 하다
role	圐 역할
take a look	보다
symphony	圐 교향곡
remain	圐 남다
incomplete	圐 미완성의
identify	圐 확인하다, 알아보다
complete	圐 완성하다
high-tech	圐 첨단 기술의
beneath	圐 ~ 아래에
recreate	圐 되살리다, 재현하다
outline	圐 윤곽
recover	圐 되찾다; 원상복구 하다
bring ~ to life	~에 생기를 불어넣다
artwork	圐 예술작품
surely	圐 확실히
expand	圐 확장하다
imaginary	圐 상상에만 존재하는, 가상의
popularity	圐 인기
forbidden	圐 금지된
expose	圐 드러내다
animate	圐 생기를 불어넣다; 만화로 만들다
unknown	圐 알려지지 않은
constantly	圐 끊임없이

evolve	통 진화하다
figure out	알아내다
achieve	통 달성하다
specific	형 특정한
goal	명 목표
knowledge	명 지식
select	형 엄선된
meet	통 만나다; 만족시키다
need	명 (~s) 요구
translate	통 번역하다
detect	통 감지하다
diagnose	통 진단하다
treat	통 치료하다
illness	명 질병
take over	넘겨받다; 대신하다
annoying	형 성가신
categorize	통 분류하다
disaster	명 재난, 재앙

UNIT 10 *Teens*

sweat	명 땀 통 땀 흘리다
beat	통 (심장 등이) 뛰다

nervous	휑 불안해하는, 초조해하는
normal	휑 정상적인, 보통인
reduce	동 줄이다
anxiety	명 불안(증)
sign	명 신호
active	휑 적극적인, 의욕적인
approach	명 접근(법) 동 접근하다
remind	동 생각나게 하다
watch out for	~을 경계하다[조심하다]
negative	휑 부정적인
replace A with B	A를 B로 대체하다
positive	휑 긍정적인
relax	동 긴장을 풀다, 쉬다
material	명 자료, 재료
turn A into B	A를 B로 바꿔놓다
release	동 방출하다; (긴장 등을) 풀다
performance	명 수행; 성적, 성과
get rid of	~을 제거하다
have nothing to do with	~와 아무런 관계가 없다
advice	명 조언, 충고
stay up all night	밤을 꼴딱 새우다
review	명 복습하다, 검토하다
work out	운동하다
extreme	휑 극심한

technique	몡 기법
focused	몡 집중한
management	몡 관리
manage	몡 관리하다
concentration	몡 집중력
divide	몡 나누다
take a break	휴식을 취하다
represent	몡 나타내다
process	몡 처리하다
anxious	몡 긴장한, 불안해하는
break down	~을 나누다

UNIT 11 The Environment

climate change	기후 변화
climate	몡 기후
refugee	몡 피난자, 난민
homeland	몡 고국, 모국
cause	몡 원인 몡 야기하다, 일으키다
pollution	몡 오염
developed country	선진국
responsible	몡 책임이 있는
affect	몡 영향을 미치다

include	⑧ 포함하다
sea level	해수면
sink	⑧ 가라앉다
in addition to	~와 더불어
storm	⑲ 폭풍우
escape	⑧ 도망치다, 피하다
face	⑲ 얼굴 ⑧ 직면하다
solve	⑧ 해결하다
harm	⑲ 해, 피해 ⑧ 해치다
give up on	~에 대해 포기하다
take responsibility for	~에 대해 책임을 지다
call	⑲ 요청, 요구
minister	⑲ 장관
urge	⑧ 촉구하다
raise	⑧ 불러일으키다
awareness	⑲ 인식
nation	⑲ 국가
deliver	⑧ 배달하다; (연설, 강연 등을) 하다
speech	⑲ 연설
knee-deep	⑱ 무릎까지 올라오는, 무릎까지 잠긴
low-lying	⑱ 낮은, 저지대의
plead	⑧ 애원하다
ancestor	⑲ 조상
issue	⑲ 문제

unsolved	혱 해결되지 않은
take action	조치를 취하다, 행동에 옮기다
immediate	혱 즉각적인

UNIT 12 *Literature*

sailor	몡 선원
destroy	동 파괴하다
prepare for	~을 준비하다
untie	동 풀다
suddenly	붸 갑자기
stream	몡 시내, 개울
chase	동 뒤쫓다
shout	동 소리지르다
shoot	동 (총, 화살 등을) 쏘다
straight	붸 똑바로
frightened	혱 깜짝 놀란, 겁에 질린
run away	도망치다
nearby	붸 가까이에
gently	붸 상냥하게
tell	동 말하다; 알다, 판단하다
save	동 저축하다; 절약하다; 구하다
lead	동 이끌다, 인도하다

share	(동) 공유하다, 나누다
enemy	(명) 적
pirate	(명) 해적
relieved	(형) 안심한
disappointed	(형) 실망한
alone	(형) 혼자, 외로운
novel	(명) 소설
captain	(명) 선장
rescue	(동) 구조하다
in honor of	~을 기념하여
character	(명) 성격; (소설 등의) 등장인물
inspire	(동) 영감을 주다
legend	(명) 전설
be based on	~에 근거하다

UNIT 13 Science

nonsense	(명) 허튼소리
sense	(명) 감각 (동) 느끼다
synesthesia	(명) 공감각
mixing	(명) 혼합
mix	(동) 혼합하다
sight	(명) 시각, 시력

report	⑧ 보고하다
automatically	⑨ 자동적으로
despite	⑳ ~에도 불구하고
confusion	⑱ 혼동, 착각
be supposed to	~하기로 되어 있다
belong to	~에 속하다
connection	⑱ 연결
disappear	⑧ 사라지다
creative	⑲ 창의적인
unique	⑲ 독특한
birth	⑱ 탄생, 출생
so far	지금까지
memorize	⑧ 암기하다
mention	⑧ 언급하다
poetry	⑱ (문학) 시
poet	⑱ 시인
term	⑱ 용어; 학기, 기간
metallic	⑲ 금속성의
tend to-v	~하는 경향이 있다
connect	⑧ 연결하다, 관련지어 생각하다
tone	⑱ 음조, 음색
particular	⑲ 특정한; 특별한
silky	⑲ 부드러운, 비단 같은
in general	일반적으로

light	혱 밝은; 가벼운

UNIT 14 *The Economy*

product	몡 상품
choose	통 선택하다
marketer	몡 마케팅 담당자
customer	몡 손님, 고객
hunger	몡 배고픔; 갈구
strategy	몡 계획, 전략
attractive	혱 매력적인
introduce	통 소개하다; (상품 등을) 내놓다
demand	몡 요구; 수요
supply	몡 공급(량)
profit	몡 이익, 수익
profitable	혱 수익성 있는
opinion	몡 의견; 여론
successfully	퇴 성공적으로
carefully	퇴 주의하여, 신중하게
control	통 지배하다; 제한하다
manufacturer	몡 제조자, 제조사
slightly	퇴 약간, 조금
competition	몡 경쟁

high-tech	형 첨단 기술의
for fun	재미로
advertisement	명 광고
appear	동 나타나다
miss	동 놓치다; 그리워하다
sell out	다 팔리다, 매진되다
fool	동 속이다, 기만하다
focus on	~에 초점을 맞추다
lack	동 부족하다
incredibly	부 믿을 수 없을 정도로, 엄청나게
wisely	부 현명하게
opportunity	명 기회
deal	명 거래, 합의
thoughtless	형 생각 없는, 무분별한
unnecessary	형 불필요한
purchase	명 구매

UNIT 15 *Health*

lose weight	살이 빠지다
weight	명 체중
commercial	명 상업 광고 형 상업의
caffeine	명 카페인

fat	⑲ 지방
regular	⑱ 규칙적인; 일상의
regularly	⑭ 규칙적으로
nutritious	⑱ 영양가 있는
contain	⑧ 포함하다
calorie	⑲ 열량
count	⑲ 총수, 총계 ⑧ 세다
athlete	⑲ 운동선수
ordinary	⑱ 평범한, 보통의
gain	⑲ 증가 ⑧ 획득하다; 증가하다
occasional	⑱ 이따금의, 가끔의
physical	⑱ 신체적인
activity	⑲ 활동
benefit	⑲ 이익, 이득
source	⑲ 근본, 원인; 원천
value	⑲ 가치
bitter	⑱ (맛이) 쓴
venture	⑧ 과감히 ~하다
nutrition	⑲ 영양(물)
label	⑲ 표, 라벨
serving	⑲ 한 끼분의 음식
amount	⑲ 양, 분량
normally	⑭ 보통, 통상적으로
equal	⑱ 똑같은 ⑧ ~와 같다

container	똉 용기, 그릇
double	휑 두 배의 똉 ~을 두 배로 하다
nutrient	똉 영양분, 영양소
daily	휑 매일의
consider	똉 고려하다; 여기다
sodium	똉 나트륨
saturated fat	포화지방
trans fat	트랜스 지방
cholesterol	똉 콜레스테롤
carbohydrate	똉 탄수화물
dietary fiber	식이섬유
protein	똉 단백질
iron	똉 철, 쇠; 철분

UNIT 16 Culture

regatta	똉 보트[요트] 경주
dried-up	휑 바싹 마른
local	휑 지방의, 지역의
raise	똉 올리다; 모으다
charity	똉 자선(단체)
entertaining	휑 재미있는
celebration	똉 축하, 축제

silly	🔞 바보 같은
main	🔞 주요한
bottom	🔞 밑바닥
cheer	🔞 환호하다, 응원하다
finish line	결승선
afterwards	🔞 뒤에, 나중에
shovel	🔞 삽
oar	🔞 노
battleship	🔞 전함
decorate	🔞 장식하다
flour	🔞 밀가루
bomb	🔞 폭탄
cannon	🔞 대포
draw	🔞 당기다; 끌다, 매혹하다
crowd	🔞 군중
forward	🔞 앞으로
strengthen	🔞 강화하다
rowing	🔞 배젓기; 조정
last	🔞 지속하다
compete	🔞 경쟁하다
competition	🔞 경쟁; 경기, 대회
beforehand	🔞 이전에, 미리
place	🔞 장소; (선수로서의) 자격
up to	~에 이르는

attraction	명 매력적인 것, 볼거리
attract	동 (흥미를) 끌다, 매혹하다
royal	형 왕[여왕]의, 왕실의

UNIT 17 Issues

various	형 다양한
profile	명 프로필, 인물 소개
post	동 (인터넷에) 게시하다, 올리다
delete	동 삭제하다
copy	동 복사하다
save	동 저장하다
inappropriate	형 부적절한
material	명 물질; 자료
arrest	동 체포하다
content	명 내용
make sure	확실하게 하다
step	명 걸음; 조치, 방법
private	형 사적인; 비공개의
etiquette	명 예의, 에티켓
hurt	동 다치게 하다; ~을 해치다
public	형 공공의; 공개적인
rumor	명 소문

characteristic	몡 특성
avoid	동 피하다
cautious	톙 조심스러운, 신중한
popularity	몡 인기
cyberbullying	몡 사이버폭력
spread	동 퍼지다
bully	동 괴롭히다 몡 괴롭히는 사람
speak out	거리낌 없이 말하다
victim	몡 피해자, 희생자
threatening	톙 위협하는
password	몡 비밀번호

UNIT 18 *Entertainment*

witch	몡 마녀
wizard	몡 마법사
mean	톙 못된, 심술궂은
character	몡 성격, 기질; 등장인물
be based on	~에 근거하다[기초하다]
inspire	동 영감을 주다
exactly	붸 정확히, 틀림없이
untold	톙 밝혀지지 않은
unlikely	톙 ~할 것 같지 않은; 예상 밖의

moving	휑 감동시키는
storyline	명 줄거리
memorable	휑 기억할 만한
major	휑 주요한, 중대한
award	명 상
success	명 성공
outstanding	휑 뛰어난
event	명 사건, 일
viewer	명 시청자, 관람객
judge	동 판단하다, 평가하다
unfairly	분 불공평하게
course	명 강의; 추이, 전개
stand up for	~을 옹호하다
injustice	명 불평등, 부당함
realize	동 깨닫다, 알아차리다
wonder	명 놀라움
impressive	휑 인상적인, 감명 깊은
worm	명 벌레
feather	명 깃털
flock	동 모이다
frequently	분 자주, 흔히
run	동 (얼마의 기간 동안) 계속되다
performance	명 공연; 성과
perform	동 수행하다; 공연하다

break	명 휴식
set	명 무대 장치[세트]
costume	명 의상, 복장
transport	동 수송하다; 데려다주다
magical	형 마법의
in no time	당장에
take ~ into consideration	~을 고려하다
scare	동 겁먹게[놀라게] 하다
in general	전반적으로
delightful	형 정말 기분 좋은, 마음에 드는
scene	명 장면

UNIT 19 *Space*

the Soviets	소련
desert	명 사막
spacecraft	명 우주선 (= craft)
launch	동 (우주선 등을) 발사하다
record	동 기록하다
control	명 통제 동 통제하다
flight	명 비행
gravity	명 중력
pass out	기절하다

ground	몧 땅, 지면
get to-v	~하게 되다
major	몧 소령
air force	공군
select	동 선택하다, 뽑다
partly	부 부분적으로
fit	동 (크기 등이) 맞다
easygoing	형 (성격이) 낙천적인, 원만한
go through	~을 겪다
historic	형 역사적으로 중요한
encourage	동 권장하다, 촉진하다
survive	동 ~에서 살아남다
astronaut	몧 우주 비행사
manned	형 (우주선 등이) 유인의
messenger	몧 (문서 등의) 배달인; 전달자, 사신
cosmos	몧 우주
height	몧 키
wonder	동 궁금해하다
walnut	몧 호두
burn	동 태우다
metal	몧 금속
spacewalk	몧 우주 유영
mix	몧 혼합(물)
theory	몧 이론

suggest	통 제안하다
chemical	명 화학 물질
drift	통 떠다니다
universe	명 우주
take part in	~에 참여[참가]하다
creation	명 생성
planet	명 행성
coal	명 석탄
release	통 방출하다
smelly	형 냄새 나는, 악취가 나는

UNIT 20 The Arts

army	명 군대; 육군
capture	통 붙잡다; 점령하다
surrender	통 항복하다
right away	당장
honor	통 ~에게 경의를 표하다
statue	명 동상
hire	통 고용하다
sculptor	명 조각가
sculpture	명 조각
of the time	그 당시의

pleased	혱 기쁜, 만족해하는
proud	혱 자랑스러운, 당당한
heroic	혱 영웅적인
hero	몡 영웅
afraid	혱 두려워하는
base	몡 기반, 토대
debate	몡 논쟁, 토론
remain	동 남다
masterpiece	몡 걸작, 명작
tragic	혱 비극적인
touching	혱 감동적인
humorous	혱 재미있는
mysterious	혱 불가사의한
historical	혱 역사상의
courageous	혱 용기 있는
prevent	동 막다
career	몡 경력, 이력
accept	동 받아들이다
support	동 부양하다
decorative	혱 장식용의
stonework	몡 돌 세공; 석조물
talented	혱 재능 있는
hell	몡 지옥
realism	몡 사실주의, 리얼리즘

| passion | 명 열정 |
| weakness | 명 약점 |

MEMO

JUNIOR READING EXPERT

A Theme-Based Reading Course for Young EFL Learners

Level 4

Answer Key

NE_ Neungyule

JUNIOR
READING EXPERT

A Theme-Based Reading Course for Young EFL Learners

Answer Key

Level 4

Before Reading | I say "OK" or "sure".

1 ③   **2** make fun of people with bad spelling   **3** ①   **4** ②   **5** ②   **6** (1) F (2) T

해석

'OK'라는 단어는 세계에서 가장 흔하게 사용되는 단어들 중 하나이다. 그것이 꽤 새로운 단어임에도 불구하고, 그것의 기원은 오랫동안 미스터리로 남아 있었다. 어떤 사람들은 그것이 '모든 것이 좋다'라는 뜻의 그리스어 'ola kala'에서 왔다고 믿었다. 다른 사람들은 그것이 아메리카 원주민 단어 'okeh'에서 왔다고 생각했다. 하지만, 그것의 진짜 기원은 마침내 1960년대에 앨런 리드라는 언어학자에 의해 밝혀졌다.

리드는 'OK'라는 단어가 사실 '보스턴 모닝 포스트'의 편집자인 찰스 고든 그린에게서 유래되었다는 것을 발견했다. 1839년에 그린은 철자를 잘못 쓰는 사람들을 놀리기 위해 'OK'라는 단어를 만들었다. 그는 'OK'가 'oll korrect'를 의미한다고 농담했는데, 이것은 'all correct'의 잘못된 철자법이다. 보통 이것과 같은 약한 농담은 금방 잊혀진다. 하지만, 'OK'라는 단어는 운이 좋았다.

1840년, 마틴 밴 뷰런은 미국 대통령으로서 재선에 출마했다. 그는 킨더훅이라는 마을에서 자랐기 때문에, 그에게는 '올드 킨더훅 (Old Kinderhook)'이라는 별명이 붙여졌다. 그의 선거 운동 동안, 지지자들은 그 별명을 'OK'로 줄였고 집회에서 "OK에 투표하라"를 외쳤다. (그 당시 모든 유명한 정치인들은 흥미로운 별명들을 가지고 있었다.) 그들은 심지어 그를 지지하기 위해 'O.K. 클럽'을 시작했다. 그 결과, 'OK'는 미국 전역으로 퍼졌고, 결국 전 세계로 퍼졌다.

요즘, 사람들은 '올드 킨더훅'에 대해서는 거의 잊어버렸다. 하지만, 'OK'라는 단어는 여전히 사람들에게 동의하는 방법으로써 '모두 옳다'라는 의미로 사용되고 있다.

어휘

commonly 📖보통, 흔히   fairly 📖꽤, 상당히   origin 🏷️기원   mystery 🏷️수수께끼, 미스터리   come from 유래하다   reveal 💬드러내다, 밝히다   language 🏷️언어   scholar 🏷️학자   discover 💬발견하다   editor 🏷️편집자   make fun of ～을 놀리다   spelling 🏷️철자법, 맞춤법   joke 💬놀리다, 농담하다 🏷️농담   incorrect 🔖부정확한   correct 🔖정확한 💬바로잡다, 정정하다   run for ～에 입후보하다   reelection 🏷️재선   president 🏷️대통령   nickname 🏷️별명   campaign 🏷️캠페인, 선거 운동   supporter 🏷️지지자 (support 💬지지하다)   shorten 💬짧게 하다   chant 💬구호를 외치다   vote 💬투표하다   rally 🏷️집회, 대회   politician 🏷️정치인, 정치가   [문제] history 🏷️역사   originate 💬비롯되다, 유래하다

구문 해설

1행   The word "OK" is **one of** the most commonly used **words** in the world.
· one of + 복수명사: ～중의 하나

6행 However, its true origin **was** finally **revealed** in the 1960s by <u>a language scholar</u> [*named* Allen Read].

- was revealed: '밝혀지다'라는 뜻으로 'be동사 + 과거분사' 형태의 수동태
- named 이하는 a language scholar를 수식하는 과거분사구

11행 He joked that "OK" meant "oll korrect," **which** is an incorrect spelling of "all correct."

- which: "oll korrect"를 선행사로 하는 계속적 용법의 주격 관계대명사

22행 However, the word "OK" **is** still **used to mean** "all correct" as <u>a way</u> [**to agree** with people].

- be used to-v: ~하는 데 사용되다 (*cf.* be used to v-ing: ~하는 데 익숙하다)
- to agree: a way를 수식하는 형용사적 용법의 to부정사

Reading 2	p.10

①

해석

우리는 많은 이유로 'goodbye'라는 단어를 말한다. 그런데 이것은 어디에서 온 것일까? 'goodbye'의 첫 번째로 알려진 사용은 1573년 가브리엘 하비라는 영국 작가가 쓴 편지에 쓰였다. 하지만, 그는 그것을 'godbwyes'라는 철자로 썼고 '신이 당신과 함께 하길'이라는 의미로 사용했다. 그 당시, 이것은 흔한 문구였다. 사람들은 먼 거리에서 의사소통할 수 없었기 때문에, 그들은 작별할 때 신에게 사랑하는 사람들과 함께 있어 달라고 부탁하곤 했다. 그러나 시간이 지나면서, 아마도 'good day'나 'good evening'과 같은 문구들 때문에, 사람들은 'God' 대신에 'good'으로 말하기 시작했다. 또한 기술이 발전함에 따라 의사소통이 더 쉬워져서, 본래의 의미는 덜 필요한 듯했다. 하지만 비록 의미가 바뀌었다고 해도, 우리는 여전히 다시 볼 때까지 사람들이 잘 지내기를 기원하기 위해 'goodbye'를 사용한다.

어휘

reason 똉이유   spell 똉철자를 쓰다   common 똉흔한   phrase 똉구절   communicate 똉의사소통하다 (communication 똉의사소통)   distance 똉거리   likely 똉아마도   technology 똉기술   advance 똉증진되다, 진전을 보이다   original 똉원래의   necessary 똉필요한   [문제] influence 똉영향

구문 해설

7행 ..., so they would **ask God to be** with their loved *ones* when they said goodbye.

- ask + 목적어 + to-v: ~에게 …해달라고 부탁하다
- one(s): 일반 사람(들)을 나타내는 부정대명사

11행 But **even though** the meaning *has changed*, we still use "goodbye" **to wish** people well until we see them again.

- even though: '~에도 불구하고'라는 의미의 부사절을 이끄는 접속사
- has changed: '결과'를 나타내는 현재완료 시제로 '~해버렸다'의 의미
- to wish: '~하기 위하여'의 의미로 목적을 나타내는 부사적 용법의 to부정사

3

A   Reading 1   origin, spelling, supporters, spread   Reading 2   changed

B   **1** origin   **2** phrase   **3** spell   **4** history   **5** necessary   **6** scholar

Reading 1 해석

앨런 리드에 의해 발견되기 전까지는 아무도 'OK'라는 단어의 진짜 기원을 알지 못했다. 그것은 몇몇 사람들이 생각했던 것처럼 그리스어나 아메리카 원주민 단어에서 나온 것이 아니다. 대신 'all correct'를 'oll korrect'로 잘못 표기해서, 철자를 잘못 쓰는 사람들을 놀리기 위해 만들어졌다. 'OK'는 한 미국 정치인이 대통령 선거에 다시 출마했을 때 유명해졌다. 그는 '올드 킨더훅(Old Kinderhook)'이라는 별명으로 불렸기 때문에, 그의 지지자들은 종종 그를 'OK'라고 부르곤 했다. 그 단어는 퍼졌고, 이제 그것은 사람들의 의견에 동의하는 흔한 방법이다!

Reading 2 해석

'godbwyes'라는 단어는 1573년 '신이 당신과 함께 하길'이라는 뜻으로 처음 사용됐지만, 시간이 흐르면서 바뀌었고 'goodbye'라는 단어가 되었다.

UNIT 02 *Society*

Reading 1   pp.12-13

Before Reading   It's because they can protect us regardless of who we are and where we come from.

1 ①   **2** help free innocent prisoners around the world   **3** ④   **4** ①   **5** ④   **6** ③

해석

매년 세계 인권 선언 기념일인 12월 10일을 시작으로 당신은 편지쓰기 캠페인(Write for Rights)에 참가할 수 있다. 일주일 동안 30개 이상의 나라에서 수만 명의 사람들이 전 세계의 무고한 수감자들을 석방하는 것을 돕기 위해 편지를 쓴다. 그 행사는 유명한 국제 인권 단체인 국제앰네스티에 의해 개최된다.

그렇다면, 편지를 쓰는 것이 어떻게 무고한 수감자들을 석방할 수 있는 걸까? 자, 편지들은 그들의 감옥에 무고한 수감자들을 가두고 있는 정부들에게 보내진다. 그런 수감자들 중 다수는 인권에 관해서 거리낌 없이 말한 것 때문에 감옥에 보내진 변호사나 언론인들이다. 편지쓰기 캠페인 주간 동안, 수십만 통의 편지가 동시에 보내진다. 그것들은 종종 커다란 상자에 담겨 모두 동시에 도착한다. 그런 식으로 정부들은 그것들을 인식하게 되는 것이다! 이 편지들 덕분에, 이미 많은 수감자들이 감옥에서 석방되었다.

누구라도 편지쓰기 캠페인에 참가할 수 있다. 당신은 심지어 당신 자신만의 편지쓰기 캠페인 행사를 열 수도 있다! 국제앰네스티 홈페이지에 방문해서 정보가 담긴 파일을 다운로드해라. 그러고 나서 도서관이나 당신의 학교와 같은 장소를 정하고 친구들과 반 친구들을 초대해서 함께 모여서 편지를 쓰는 것이다. (반 친구들을 초대하는 것은 우정을 쌓는 좋은 방법이다.) 편지쓰기 캠페인은 인권 보호를 위해 함께 일할 수 있는 훌륭한 기회이다.

구문 해설

3행 ..., tens of thousands of people in more than thirty countries write letters to help free ...

주어 / 동사

• help + (to) 동사원형: ~하는 것을 돕다

10행 ... lawyers or journalists [who were put in jail for speaking out about human rights].

• who: lawyers or journalists를 수식하는 주격 관계대명사
• for: 이유, 원인을 나타내는 전치사

14행 Thanks to these letters, many prisoners have already been freed from jail.

• thanks to: ~ 덕분에
• have been freed: '완료'를 나타내는 현재완료 수동태

Reading 2   p.14

①

해석

관계자님께,

자신의 국토와 민족을 위해 싸운 Manuel Morales는 과테말라 사람들에게 영웅입니다. 현재 Cahabón 강과 그 주변의 땅은 발전소 건설로 인해 죽어가고 있습니다. 이 지역들은 과테말라 문화와 일상생활에 중요합니다. 이전에, Manuel과 그의 마을 사람들은 이러한 파괴로부터 땅과 물을 보호하기 위해 함께 일했습니다. Manuel은 과테말라의 미래를 위해 평화롭게 싸웠음에도, 그는 체포되어 7년째 감옥에 있습니다. 거짓 증거가 그를 그곳에 가두는 데 사용되었습니다. 그는 아무 잘못된 행동도 하지 않았기 때문에, 이것은 완전히 불공평합니다. 당신은 반드시 옳은 일을 해야 하고, 그를 즉시 감옥에서 석방해야 합니다.

진심으로,

엘레나로부터

destruction 명파괴   peacefully 부평화롭게   future 명미래   arrest 동체포하다   false 형잘못된, 거짓의
evidence 명증거   completely 부완전히   unfair 형불공평한   release 동석방하다   prison 명감옥   immediately
부즉시   [문제] demand 동요구하다   apologize 동사과하다   behavior 명행동   forgiveness 명용서   slow down
늦추다

2행   Manuel Morales, [**who** fought for his land and people], is a hero to Guatemalans.
            주어   동사
     • who가 이끄는 삽입절은 Manuel Morales를 부연 설명하는 주격 관계대명사절

6행   **Though** Manuel fought peacefully ..., he ┌ was arrested
                                                   │ and
                                                   └ has been in jail for seven years now.

     • though: '~함에도 불구하고'라는 의미의 부사절을 이끄는 접속사

8행   This is completely unfair, **as** he has done *nothing wrong*.
     • as: 《이유》 ~하기 때문에
     • -thing으로 끝나는 대명사를 수식할 때는 형용사가 그 뒤에 위치함

Unit Review   p.15

A   [Reading 1]   organizes, governments, prisoners, protect   [Reading 2]   released
B   **1** apologize   **2** construction   **3** innocent   **4** protect   **5** organize   **6** hero

Reading 1 해석

매년 12월 10일부터 17일까지, 국제앰네스티는 편지쓰기 캠페인을 개최한다. 이 행사의 목적은 편지를 써서 전 세계의 무고한 수감자들을 석방하는 것이다. 매년, 수천 통의 편지가 감옥에 무고한 사람이 있는 정부들에게 보내진다. 그리고 많은 수감자들이 이 편지들 때문에 석방되었다. 이 행사에 참가하기 위해서는 국제앰네스티 홈페이지에서 정보가 담긴 파일을 다운로드해라. 그리고 친구들이나 반 친구들과 함께 모여서 편지를 써라! 그것은 인권을 보호하기 위한 좋은 방법이다.

Reading 2 해석

글쓴이는 Manuel Morales가 Cahabón 강 지역을 지키기 위해 평화롭게 싸웠고 부당하게 감옥에 갇혔기 때문에 석방돼야 한다고 주장한다.

Reading 1   pp.16-17

Before Reading As many desserts come from France, I guess pretzels were also created in France.

1 ②   **2** a child's arms folded to pray   **3** ④   **4** ③   **5** ②   **6** (1) F (2) T

해석

프레첼(pretzel)은 밀가루 반죽으로 만들어진 맛있는 간식이다. 그것들 중 어떤 것은 빵처럼 부드럽고, 또 어떤 것은 쿠키처럼 딱딱하다. 당신은 프레첼을 모양으로 알아볼 수 있는데, 그것은 매듭처럼 꼬여 있다. 프레첼은 원래 유럽에서 왔지만, 그것들은 이제 미국에서 가장 인기 있는 과자 중 하나이다. 여러분은 제과점에서, 극장에서, 그리고 스포츠 행사에서 그것들을 파는 것을 볼 수 있다.

프레첼은 7세기 프랑스 남부에서 만들어졌다. 어느 날 수도사 몇 명이 빵을 굽고 있었다. 수도사들 중 한 사람은 그의 빵을 기도하려고 굽힌 아이의 팔 모양으로 만들기로 했다. 이 수도사는 그 특별한 빵 몇 개를 착하게 행동하고 기도를 한 보상으로 어린이들에게 주었다. 그래서 이 꼬여 있는 과자는 라틴어로 '작은 보상'이라는 뜻의 '프레티올라(pretiola)'라고 별명이 붙여졌다. 프레티올라는 곧 유럽 전체에서 인기를 얻었고, 이름이 '프레첼(pretzel)'로 바뀌었다. 나중에, 프레첼은 초기 정착민들의 배에 실려 미국으로 전해졌다. 미국에서 첫 번째 프레첼 빵집이 문을 연 곳은 바로 펜실베이니아였다.

오늘날 오스트리아에서는 사람들이 아침 식사로 프레첼을 먹는다. 독일과 스위스에서는 프레첼을 잘라서 벌려 거기에 버터를 바른다. 미국에서 여러분은 여러 가지 다른 맛의 프레첼을 먹어볼 수 있다! 부드러운 프레첼의 종류로는 달콤한 계피, 참깨, 마늘 버터, 그리고 허니 머스터드가 있다. 몇몇 딱딱한 프레첼은 요구르트나 초콜릿으로 덮여 있다. 여러분이 단 것을 좋아하든 짠 것을 좋아하든, 부드러운 것을 좋아하든 딱딱한 것을 좋아하든, 프레첼은 확실히 맛있는 '작은 보상'이다!

어휘

treat 圀 만족[즐거움]을 주는 것   wheat flour 밀가루   dough 圀 반죽   recognize 圄 알아보다   twist 圄 꼬다, 감다 knot 圀 매듭   originally 凰 원래, 처음에는   for sale 팔려고 내놓은   monk 圀 수도사, 승려   fold 圄 접다, 구부리다   pray 圄 기도하다   reward 圀 보상, 사례   settler 圀 이주자, 정착민   variety 圀 다양(성); *종류   cinnamon 圀 계피   sesame 圀 참깨   cover 圄 덮다, 바르다   certainly 凰 확실히   [문제] advantage 圀 이점, 이익   flavor 圀 맛, 풍미

구문 해설

3행   You can recognize pretzels by their shape, **which** is twisted like a knot.
         • which: their shape을 선행사로 하는 계속적 용법의 주격 관계대명사로, and it으로 바꾸어 쓸 수 있음

10행   **One of** the **monks** decided ... in the shape of a child's arms [*folded* to pray].
         • one of + 복수명사: ~중의 하나
         • folded 이하는 a child's arms를 수식하는 과거분사구

11행   This monk **gave** <u>some of the special bread</u> **to** <u>children</u> *for* being good and praying.

                                    A   B

- give A to B: give B A로 바꾸어 쓸 수 있음 (= gave children some of the special bread)
- for: 《보수·대상》 ~에 대해서, ~의 보답으로

Reading 2   p.18

⑤

해석

딱딱한 프레첼은 1700년대 후반 미국의 펜실베이니아에서 실수로 만들어졌다. 어느 날, 제빵사의 조수가 불 위에서 프레첼을 굽던 중에 잠이 들었다. (C) 그 결과, 그는 프레첼을 평소보다 두 배나 오래 구웠다. 그 주인 제빵사는 돌아와 무슨 일이 일어났는지를 보고는 자신의 조수에게 소리를 질렀다. (B) 그러나, 프레첼을 버리던 중에 그는 하나를 맛보았다. 너무 구워진 프레첼은 딱딱하고, 바삭바삭하고, 그리고 맛있었다! 주인 제빵사는 깜짝 놀랐다. (A) 그 딱딱한 프레첼은 맛있었을 뿐만 아니라 건조했기 때문에 더 오래 보관될 수 있었다. 딱딱한 프레첼은 이제 부드러운 것만큼이나 인기 있다!

어휘

by mistake 실수로   late 휑 늦은; *후반의   helper 몡 도와주는 사람, 조수   tasty 휑 맛있는 (taste 동 맛보다)   store 동 저장하다   throw out 내던지다. 버리다   overcooked 휑 지나치게[너무] 구워진   crunchy 휑 바삭바삭한   master 몡 주인 shout 동 소리를 지르다

구문 해설

4행   **Not only** <u>were</u> <u>the hard pretzels</u> tasty, **but** they could be stored longer …

                      동사   주어

- not only A but (also) B: A뿐만 아니라 B도
- 부정어(Not only)가 문장 앞에 오면서 주어와 동사가 도치됨

8행   As a result, he baked the pretzels **for** *twice as long as* usual.

- for: 《시간》 ~동안
- 배수사 + as + 형용사/부사 + as: ~배만큼 …한/하게

Unit Review   p.19

A   Reading 1   praying, spreads, settlers, varieties   Reading 2   mistake

B   **1** twist   **2** settler   **3** reward   **4** dough   **5** crunchy   **6** shout

Reading 2 해석

어느 조수의 프레첼을 너무 오랫동안 굽는 <u>실수</u> 덕분에, 우리는 오늘날 딱딱한 프레첼을 즐길 수 있다.

Reading 1   pp.20-21

Before Reading I think taxi drivers and store cashiers will be replaced by machines in the future.

1 ③ **2** ③, ④ **3** ④ **4** ① **5** ② **6** recording speech

해석

과거에 흔했던 많은 직업들이 더 이상 존재하지 않는다. 어떤 것들은 생활 방식의 변화 때문에 사라졌고, 다른 것들은 발전한 기술로 인해 불필요해졌다. 몇 가지 예를 살펴보자.

1600년대에, 어떤 사람들은 약초 뿌리는 사람으로 일했다. 부유한 가정들은 그들의 집 주변에 약초와 꽃을 뿌리기 위해 그들을 고용했다. 그 당시에, 제대로 된 비누는 비쌌고, 집에는 (수도) 배관이나 뜨거운 물이 없었다. 이것은 사람들이 목욕을 자주 하는 것을 어렵게 만들었다. 그래서 약초와 꽃들은 그들의 나쁜 냄새를 감추기 위해 사용되었다! 오늘날, 대부분의 사람들은 뜨거운 물과 비누에 접근할 수 있기 때문에 약초 뿌리는 사람은 더 이상 존재하지 않는다.

얼음을 자르는 것은 더 이상 필요하지 않은 또 다른 일이다. 냉장고 (발명) 이전에, 얼음은 구하기 어려웠다. 그래서 얼음을 자르는 사람들은 얼어붙은 호수에서 얼음덩어리를 잘라내기 위해 마력으로 작동하는 기구를 사용하곤 했다. 극한의 기후 조건에 직면해야 했기 때문에 이 일은 상당히 어려웠다. 그러나 현대 냉장고가 발명된 <u>이후로</u>, 얼음을 자르는 사람들은 더 이상 필요하지 않게 되었다.

마지막으로, 회사들은 더 이상 전문 타이피스트를 필요로 하지 않는다. 컴퓨터가 발명되기 전에, 회사들은 그들의 문서를 타이핑하기 위해 많은 타이피스트를 고용할 필요가 있었다. 하지만 오늘날, 컴퓨터는 이 일을 완전히 불필요하게 만들었다. 사실, 컴퓨터는 심지어 말을 녹음하여 문서를 만들 수도 있다!

세상이 변하고 기술이 발전함에 따라, 더 많은 직업이 불필요해질 것이다. 여러분은 다음에는 어떤 직업이 사라질 것 같은가?

어휘

exist 동 존재하다   disappear 동 사라지다   lifestyle 명 생활 방식   unnecessary 형 불필요한   due to ~ 때문에 herb strewer 약초 뿌리는 사람   hire 동 고용하다   spread 동 뿌리다, 흩뿌리다   proper 형 적절한, 제대로 된   plumbing 명 배관   bathe 동 목욕하다   hide 동 숨기다   have access to ~에 접근할 수 있다   no longer 더 이상 ~않은   fridge 명 냉장고   horse-powered 형 마력의   device 명 장치   face 동 직면하다   extreme 형 극도의, 극심한   invent 동 발명하다   require 동 필요로 하다, 요구하다   professional 형 전문적인   document 명 문서   [문제] replace 동 대체하다 population 명 인구   development 명 발전   rare species 희귀종   decorate 동 장식하다, 꾸미다

구문 해설

1행   Many jobs [**that** were common in the past] do not exist anymore.
　　　주어　　　　　　　　　　　　　　　　동사
- that: 선행사 Many jobs를 수식하는 주격 관계대명사

11행   This made **it** difficult **for people to bathe** often.
- it은 가목적어이고, to bathe가 진목적어이며 for people은 to부정사의 의미상 주어

So the herbs and flowers **were used to hide** their bad smell!

• be used to-v: ~하는 데 쓰이다 (*cf.* be used to v-ing: ~하는 데 익숙하다)

15행 So ice cutters **would use** a horse-powered device *to cut* blocks of ice from frozen lakes.

• would + 동사원형: ~하곤 했다 (과거의 불규칙적인 습관을 나타냄)

• to cut: '~하기 위하여'의 의미로 목적을 나타내는 부사적 용법의 to부정사

Reading 2   p.22

③

해석

미래에 로봇이 우리의 모든 일을 대체하겠는가? 답은 '아니오'이다. 이것은 많은 직업이 인간의 자질을 필요로 하기 때문이다. 예를 들어, 오직 인간만이 작가가 될 수 있다. 글쓰기는 예술의 한 형태이고, 작가들은 그들 자신의 경험, 아이디어, 그리고 상상력으로부터 내용을 만들어낸다. 그것은 어려운 작업이고, 로봇은 그것을 할 능력이 부족하다. 로봇은 변호사의 일도 할 수 없다. 변호사가 된다는 것은 많은 분석과 협상을 필요로 한다. 그들은 복잡한 법을 이해하고 고객들의 사건들을 논의할 필요가 있다. 로봇은 이런 종류의 일들을 할 수 없다. 많은 일들이 심장과 뇌를 가진 진짜 인간에 의해서만 오직 이루어질 수 있기 때문에, 로봇은 결코 노동력에서 우리를 완전히 대체할 수 없을 것이다.

어휘

quality 몡자질   content 몡내용   imagination 몡상상(력)   lack 통부족하다   ability 몡능력   involve 통수반[포함]하다, 필요로 하다   analysis 몡분석   negotiation 몡협상   complicated 형복잡한   law 몡법   argue 통논의하다   case 몡사건   client 몡고객   be capable of ~할 수 있다   workforce 몡노동력, 노동 인구   [문제] switch 통바꾸다

구문 해설

4행 It is a difficult task, and robots lack the ability [**to do** it].

• to do: '~하는'의 의미로 the ability를 수식하는 형용사적 용법의 to부정사

5행 **Being a lawyer** involves a lot of analysis and negotiation.

• Being a lawyer는 주어로 사용된 동명사구로서 3인칭 단수 취급하므로 동사는 involves를 사용함

Unit Review   p.23

A **Reading 1** spreading, access, frozen, typed, computer

B **1** imagination **2** negotiation **3** disappear **4** hire **5** face **6** professional

UNIT 05 Animals

pp.24-25

Reading 1

Before Reading I read in a book that they love fruit, leafy plants, and even bamboo.

1 ② **2** ③ **3** Gorillas eat so many different kinds of plants **4** ② **5** ① **6** ①

해석

우간다의 브윈디 국립공원 위로 해가 떠오를 때, 고릴라 가족이 잠에서 깨어나고 있다. 그들은 나뭇잎 침대에서 나와 몇 미터 떨어진 곳에 앉아 근처의 식물들을 먹기 시작한다. 고릴라들이 먹고 있는 동안, 한 과학자가 그들이 어떤 종류의 식물을 먹는지 관찰하고 있다. 왜일까? 왜냐하면 고릴라들은 천성적으로 인간의 건강에도 좋을 수 있는 먹이를 고르기 때문이다!

고릴라들의 습관에 대한 연구는 1980년대에 시작되었다. 그 당시 과학자들은 침팬지들이 배탈이 났을 때 그들이 항상 특정 식물을 먹는다는 것을 알게 되었다. 나중에 이 식물이 세균들을 죽임으로써 인간의 배탈을 치료할 수 있다는 사실이 발견되었다. 몇몇 과학자들은 약으로 작용하는 더 많은 식물들을 찾아내기 위해 동물들의 식생활을 연구하기로 결정했다. 그들은 고릴라가 아주 많은 다양한 종류의 식물을 먹기 때문에 고릴라를 선택했으며, 따라서 유용한 약을 발견할 가능성이 높아지게 된다. 숲속에서 과학자들은 고릴라들이 가장 좋아하는 먹이의 샘플을 모은다. 그런 다음 그들은 그것들의 다양한 용도를 알아내기 위해 실험한다.

지금까지 과학자들은 고릴라들이 먹기 좋아하는 71가지 서로 다른 종류의 식물을 알아냈다. 그들은 이 식물들 중 적어도 세 가지가 약일 수 있다고 생각한다. 서로 다른 모든 식물들을 실험하려면 어느 정도의 시간이 걸릴 것이다. 그러나 고릴라들 덕분에 사람들은 언젠가 이 약들의 혜택을 누릴지도 모른다.

어휘

leafy ⑬잎이 우거진; *잎으로 된   nearby ⑬근처의   observe ⑧관찰하다   naturally ⑭천성적으로   particular ⑬특정한   stomachache ⑲배탈, 복통   discover ⑧발견하다   cure ⑧치료하다   germ ⑲세균   diet ⑲식습관, (일상의) 음식물   medicine ⑲약   thus ⑭그러므로, 따라서   collect ⑧모으다   various ⑬다양한   so far 지금까지   at least 적어도   benefit from ~의 혜택을 누리다   [문제] typical ⑬전형적인   medical ⑬의학적인   effect ⑲효과

구문 해설

11행   **It** was later discovered **that** this plant can cure stomachaches in humans *by killing* germs.
- It은 가주어, that 이하는 진주어임
- by v-ing: ~함으로써

13행   They chose gorillas …, thus **the possibility of discovering** useful medicines *goes* up.

주어 ───────────── 동사
- the possibility of v-ing: ~할 가능성
- 주어가 the possibility이므로 동사는 3인칭 단수형인 goes를 씀

18행   **It will take some time to test** all the different plants.
- it takes + 시간 + to-v: ~하는 데 …의 시간이 걸리다

11

④

해석

고릴라는 많은 면에서 인간과 꼭 닮았다. 그들은 두 개의 팔과 다리, 열 개의 손가락과 발가락, 그리고 심지어 우리처럼 32개의 치아를 가지고 있다. 그들은 서로 돌보고, 먹고, 놀고, 잠자면서 그들의 하루하루를 함께 보낸다. 슬프게도, 이 아름답고 영리한 생물들은 심각한 멸종 위기에 처해 있다. 현재 극히 적은 수의 고릴라가 남아 있으며 그들은 많은 위협에 직면해 있다. 가장 큰 문제는 그들이 그들의 집을 잃어가고 있다는 것이다. 사람들은 목재를 위해 그들의 숲을 벤다. 또한 사냥꾼들은 고릴라를 죽이고 그 고기를 팔아서 돈을 벌려고 한다. 우리는 이 '온순한 거대 동물들'을 보호하기 위해 노력해야 한다. 그렇지 않으면 그들은 곧 사라질 것이고 우리는 그들의 친근한 얼굴을 다시는 볼 수 없을지도 모른다.

어휘

care for ~을 돌보다   intelligent 형 지능이 있는, 영리한   creature 명 생물   seriously 부 심각하게   endangered 형 멸종 위기에 처한   threat 명 위협   lose 동 잃다   make an effort 노력하다   friendly 형 친근한, 정다운   [문제] deal with 다루다, 대하다   critically 부 위태롭게

구문 해설

2행   They **spend** their days **caring** for one another, **eating**, **playing**, and **sleeping** together.
      • spend + 시간 + v-ing: ~하면서 …의 시간을 보내다

Unit Review   p.27

A   Reading 1   humans, eat, samples, medicines

B   **1** discover   **2** creature   **3** intelligent   **4** medicine   **5** germ   **6** threat

Reading 1 해석

1980년대에, 과학자들은 침팬지가 그들의 배탈을 치료하기 위해 한 식물을 먹고 있는 것을 보았다. 그들은 똑같은 식물이 <u>인간</u>의 배탈 또한 치료한 것을 알게 되었다. 이 때문에, 과학자들은 동물들이 무엇을 <u>먹는지</u>를 연구하는 프로젝트를 시작했다. 그들은 고릴라가 매우 다양한 식물들을 먹기 때문에 고릴라를 선택했다. 과학자들은 고릴라를 따라가서 그들이 먹는 식물들의 <u>샘플</u>들을 채취한다. 그러고 나서 그들은 그것들이 인간에게 <u>약</u>으로 사용될 수 있는지를 알아보기 위해 그것들을 가지고 실험한다. 지금까지 세 가지의 식물들이 질병을 치유하는 약으로 여겨진다.

UNIT 06 People

pp.28-29

Reading 1

Before Reading My favorite baseball player is Lee Jeong-hoo, and I am also a big fan of his team.

1 ① **2** he didn't speak English well **3** ② **4** ③ **5** ① **6** ④

해석

"만일 당신에게 상황을 더 좋게 만들 기회가 있는데 하지 않는다면, 당신은 지구에서의 시간을 낭비하고 있는 것이다."

이것은 메이저리그의 스타가 된 최초의 라틴 아메리카계 야구 선수인 로베르토 클레멘테의 말이다. 그는 푸에르토리코에서 태어났고 1955년에 메이저리그에 입성했다. 처음에 그는 영어를 잘하지 못해서 힘든 시간을 보냈다. 그러나 결국 그는 야구계의 최고 선수들 중 한 명이 되었고 월드 시리즈에서 두 번이나 우승했다. 그는 또한 1966년에는 메이저리그 최우수 선수로 지명되었다.

그러나 클레멘테는 타인들에게 관심을 가진 것으로 훨씬 더 잘 기억되고 있다. 그는 가난한 사람들을 도왔고 라틴 아메리카인들과 흑인들에 대한 일부 나쁜 생각들을 바꾸기 위해 싸웠다. 1972년 니카라과에서 끔찍한 지진이 일어났을 때 클레멘테는 직접 그곳에 가서 돕기로 결심했다. 그러나 슬프게도 원조 물자를 싣고가던 그의 비행기가 바닷속으로 추락하고 말았다. 그는 겨우 37세였고 그의 시신은 전혀 발견되지 않았다.

사망 후 클레멘테는 야구 명예의 전당에 (이름이) 추가됐다. 푸에르토리코에서는 아이들을 위한 스포츠 캠프가 그를 기념하여 만들어졌다. 그리고 매년, 다른 사람들을 돕기 위해 가장 많은 일을 하는 메이저리거가 로베르토 클레멘테 상을 받는다. 클레멘테는 진정으로 세상을 보다 더 좋은 곳으로 만든 사람이었다.

어휘

opportunity 명기회 Hispanic 형명라틴 아메리카계의 (사람) join 동가입하다, 합류하다 eventually 부결국 twice 부두 번 name 동명명하다; *지명하다 MVP (스포츠) 최우수 선수 (most valuable player) care about ~에 관심을 가지다 African-American 명형아프리카계 미국인(의) earthquake 명지진 aid 명원조, 도움 package 명꾸러미, 소포 crash 동추락하다, 충돌하다 body 명몸; *시신 Hall of Fame 명예의 전당 in one's honor ~을 기념하여 award 명상 truly 부진정으로 [문제] historic 형역사적으로 중요한 moment 명순간 tragic 형비극적인 adventurous 형모험적인 continue 동계속하다 be named after ~의 이름을 따서 이름 지어지다 save 동저장하다; *구하다

구문 해설

1행 "If you have an opportunity [**to make** things better] and you don't (make things better),

you are ... on this earth."
- to make: '~할'의 의미로 an opportunity를 수식하는 형용사적 용법의 to부정사
- you don't 뒤에는 make things better가 중복을 피하기 위해 생략되어 있음

He **was** also **named** the league's MVP in 1966.

     A   B

- A is named B: 'A를 B로 임명하다'라는 뜻인 name A B의 수동태

10행   However, Clemente is **even** better remembered for caring about others.

- even: 비교급 better를 강조하는 말로 '훨씬'의 의미이며 far, much 등으로 바꿔 쓸 수 있음

Reading 2   p.30

②

해석

로베르토 클레멘테 이전에, 미국 사회를 변화시킨 또 다른 훌륭한 야구 선수가 있었다. 1946년에 재키 로빈슨은 최초의 흑인 메이저리그 야구 선수가 되었다. 그 이전에는, 흑인들은 다른 리그에서 경기를 해야 했다. 그래서 그가 처음 메이저리그에서 경기를 하기 시작했을 때, 일부 팬들과 다른 선수들은 그를 향해 끔찍한 말들을 외쳤다. 그러나 로빈슨은 포기하지 않았다. 그는 곧 그의 멋진 경기로 모든 사람의 존경을 얻어냈다. 그는 심지어 1947년에 메이저리그의 최우수 선수로 선정되기도 했다. 머지않아 메이저리그에는 많은 다른 흑인들이 등장했다. 이것은 미국을 어떤 피부색을 가진 사람이든 살기 좋은 장소로 만들기 위한 중요한 단계였다.

어휘

yell ⑧외쳐 말하다   give up 포기하다   respect ⑲존경, 존중   terrific ⑲멋진   before long 머지않아   toward ⑳ ~을 향하여   [문제] in need 어려움에 처한   overcome ⑧극복하다   physical ⑲신체의   difficulty ⑲어려움, 곤경

구문 해설

8행   This was an important step toward **making America a great place** [to live] for people of any color.

- make + 목적어 + 목적보어: ~을 …로 만들다

Unit Review   p.31

A   Reading 1   Hispanic, won, earthquake, award

B   **1** respect   **2** join   **3** named   **4** eventually   **5** aid   **6** give up

pp.32-33

Reading 1

Before Reading I have been to Italy. I liked Rome the most because I could visit some historical places, such as the Colosseum and the Pantheon.

1 ③ **2** ② **3** ② **4** they wanted a place to pray **5** ③ **6** ③

해석

폴란드에서의 셋째 날

오늘은 폴란드에서 보내는 휴가의 셋째 날이었다. 우리는 비엘리치카 소금 광산으로 향했다. 그렇다! 그것은 금광이 아니라 소금 광산이다. 어쨌든 비엘리치카 광산은 유명한 관광 명소인데, 왜냐하면 그 깊숙한 내부에는 모두 소금으로 만들어진 조각상들, 미술관들, 교회들이 있기 때문이다! 그것은 600년도 더 되었다. 가이드는 우리에게 수백만 년 전에는 그곳에 바다가 있었다고 말해 주었다. 정말 흥미롭다!

우리는 광산으로 들어가기 위해 350개 이상의 계단을 내려갔다. 지하의 공기는 선선하고 습했다. 우리가 터널을 통해서 걸어갈 때 나는 폴란드 왕들과 왕비들의 조각상들을 보았다. 그들은 꼭 실제 사람처럼 보였다! 나는 또한 벽의 아름다운 그림들도 보았다. 굴의 일부는 교회들이었다 – 그렇다, 소금 교회들이다! 그러면 누가 이 모든 것을 만들었을까? 광부들이 만든 것이다! 19세기에 광부들은 거의 하루 종일을 지하에서 보냈다. 그들은 기도할 장소를 원했고, 그래서 광산 안에 교회들을 지었다. 오늘날에는 아름다운 소금 볼거리들로 가득 찬 3.5 킬로미터의 터널이 있다. 소금으로 만들어진 바닥, 천장, 벽, 그리고 심지어 샹들리에까지 있어 나는 꿈나라에 온 것 같은 느낌이 들었다.

관광을 마칠 때쯤 우리는 327 미터 지하에 있었다. 내 생각에 그것이 내 평생에 있어본 곳 중 가장 깊은 곳이었던 것 같다. 광산을 떠나기 위해 우리는 엘리베이터를 타고 올라갔다. 햇빛이 내 눈에 너무 밝았지만, 나는 그것을 다시 보게 되어 기뻤다.

어휘

head for ~로 향하다　mine 명광산 동캐다, 채굴하다 (miner 명광부)　tourist attraction 관광 명소 (attraction 명볼거리, 매력)　statue 명조각상　gallery 명미술관　church 명교회　step 명걸음; *계단　underground 부지하에　damp 형습기 찬, 축축한　cave 명동굴　nearly 부거의　pray 동기도하다　nowadays 부오늘날에는　be filled with ~로 가득 차다　ceiling 명천장　chandelier 명샹들리에　[문제] scared 형겁에 질린　exhausted 형지친

구문 해설

4행　... because deep inside it **are** statues, galleries, and churches—all made of salt!
　　　　　　　　부사구　　　　동사　　　　주어
　• 부사구가 문장의 앞에 오면서 주어와 동사가 도치되었으며, 이때 동사는 주어의 수에 일치시키므로 복수형 are가 쓰임

13행　Nowadays there are 3.5 km of tunnels [(which are) filled with beautiful salt attractions].
　• 선행사 tunnels와 filled 사이에는 '주격 관계대명사 + be동사'가 생략되었음

16행   I think that was <u>the deepest place</u> [(that) I have ever been in my life].

- the deepest place 뒤에는 관계부사 that이 생략된 것으로 볼 수 있음 (선행사에 최상급이 있는 경우에는 where가 아닌 that을 사용함)

Reading 2   p.34

②

해석

오늘날, 우리는 소금을 가게에서 저렴하게 살 수 있다. 그러나, 오래전에 그것은 매우 귀하게 여겨졌다. 소금은 음식을 더 맛있게 하고 우리 몸을 건강하게 유지해줄 뿐만 아니라, 음식을 보존하는 데도 도움을 준다. 그러므로, 그 당시에 소금은 오늘날보다 훨씬 더 중요했다. 하지만, 전 세계 모든 곳에 충분한 소금이 있던 것은 아니다. 이런 곳에서는 소금이 너무 귀한 물품이어서 때때로 그것은 심지어 돈으로 사용되었다. 실제로, 고대 로마에서는 군인의 월급이 소금이었다. 이것은 '샐러리움(salarium)'이라고 알려졌는데, 거기서 '샐러리(salary)'라는 단어가 유래한 것이다.

어휘

cheaply 🕮저렴하게   valuable 🕮귀중한   preserve 🕮보존하다, 보관하다   item 🕮품목   ancient 🕮고대의   soldier 🕮군인   payment 🕮지불; *보수   be known as ~라고 알려지다   salary 🕮월급, 급료   [문제] fuel 🕮연료   cleaner 🕮세제   seasoning 🕮양념

구문 해설

2행   Salt **not only** makes food taste better and keeps our bodies healthy, **but** it **also** *helps preserve* food.

- not only A but also B: A뿐만 아니라 B도 역시
- help + (to) 동사원형: ~하는 것을 돕다, ~에 도움이 되다

6행   ..., salt was **such** a valuable item **that** sometimes it was even used as money.

- such ~ that ...: 너무 ~해서 …하다

Unit Review   p.35

A   **Reading 1** attraction, sea, salt, miners   **Reading 2** valuable

B   **1** head for   **2** preserve   **3** pray   **4** mine   **5** valuable   **6** ceiling

Reading 1 해석

폴란드의 비엘리치카 소금 광산은 인기 있는 관광 명소이다. 그것은 600년 이상 되었다. 오래전에, 그 광산은 사실 바다였다. 현재 그 지하 터널은 관광객들이 방문하는 장소이다. 그 광산에 대한 놀라운 사실은 광산 안의 모든 것들이 소금으로 만들어져 있다는 것이다.

그 내부에는 조각상, 미술관, 그리고 심지어 교회도 있다. 광부들이 기도할 장소를 갖기 위해 교회를 지었다고 한다.

Reading 2 해석

오늘날과 달리, 과거에는 소금이 많은 장점과 제한된 양 때문에 믿을 수 없을 정도로 가치 있었다.

UNIT 08 *Sports*

Reading 1   pp.36-37

Before Reading Sure, I usually go to ballparks during the Korean Baseball League's regular season.

1 ①   **2** ②   **3** ②   **4** its outfield is rather small   **5** ④   **6** ②

해석

많은 요소들이 야구 경기 결과에 영향을 끼칠 수 있다. 그러나 야구장 자체가 경기가 진행되는 방식에 중요한 영향을 미친다는 것을 알고 있었는가? 대부분의 운동 경기는 모두 정확하게 똑같은 경기장에서 이루어지지만 야구는 그렇지 않다. 모든 야구장은 같은 내야 규격을 따라야 하는 반면, 외야는 각기 다르다. 그것은 각각의 경기장이 크기와 모양에 있어서 다를 수 있다는 것을 의미한다. 게다가, 어떤 경기장들은 다른 경기장들보다 더 높거나 더 낮은 담장을 가지고 있다. 그리고 어떤 경기장들은 지붕이 있지만, 어떤 것은 없다.

이런 차이들 때문에, 팀들이 많은 득점을 할 가능성이 더 높은 야구장이 있고, 대체로 낮은 득점의 경기를 보이는 야구장이 있다. 첫 번째 그룹은 '타자형 구장'이라고 알려진 반면, 두 번째 그룹은 '투수형 구장'이다. 텍사스 주의 휴스턴에 있는 애스트로스 미닛메이드 야구장은 타자형 구장이다. 그 경기장의 외야는 다소 작은데, 그래서 다른 야구장에서는 쉽게 아웃될 안타도 미닛메이드 야구장에서는 종종 홈런이 된다. 코치와 선수 모두 이런 차이들을 알고 있어서, 그들이 어느 야구장에서 시합하는지에 따라 종종 전략을 바꿀 것이다.

야구장의 독특함은 경기를 더 흥미롭게 만들어주는 어떤 것이다. 각각의 경기처럼 각각의 야구장이 다르다. 그러므로 팬들은 무슨 일이 벌어질지 결코 알 수 없다.

어휘

factor 명요인, 요소   influence 명영향 *동~에 영향을 주다   result 명결과   have an effect on ~에 영향을 미치다   field 명들판; *경기장   exactly 부정확하게   ballpark 명야구장   measurement 명측량; *치수   infield 명내야   outfield 명외야   fence 명담장   score 동득점하다, 얻다   run 명득점   hitter 명타자 (hit 명안타)   pitcher 명투수   strategy 명전략   according to ~에 따라   [문제] alike 형서로 닮은, 비슷한   in contrast 대조적으로   challenge 명도전   advantage 명이익, 강점   uniqueness 명독특함[성]

11행 ..., there are ballparks [**where** teams *are* more *likely to score* a lot of runs], ...

- where: ballparks를 수식하는 장소를 나타내는 관계부사
- be likely to-v: ~할 가능성이 있다, ~하는 경향이 있다

16행 ... they'll often change strategies according to **which park they play in**.

- which park 이하는 '그들이 어떤 야구장에서 경기하는지'라는 의미의 간접의문문으로 전치사 in을 쓰는 것에 유의해야 함 (they play in _____ park)

18행 The uniqueness of baseball parks is something [**that** *makes the sport more exciting*].

- something과 같이 -thing으로 끝나는 명사를 수식할 때는 관계대명사 that을 사용함
- make + 목적어 + 형용사: ~을 …하게 만들다

Reading 2   p.38

②

해석

당신은 아마도 야구장을 여러 번 보았을 것이다. 그러나 잘 알려지지 않은 몇몇 공간이 있다. 바로 더그아웃과 불펜이다. 더그아웃은 경기장의 측면에 있는 한 구역이다. 그 안에는 선수들이 경기 중에 앉아 있을 수 있는 벤치가 있다. 또한 선수들이 헬멧이나 방망이 같은 자신의 장비를 보관하는 공간들도 있다. (그들이 스포츠 회사로부터 모든 장비를 무료로 받는 것은 흔한 일이다.) 더그아웃의 한쪽 편에는, 보통 불펜이라고 불리는 공간이 있다. 이것은 투수들이 경기에 들어가기 전에 준비운동을 할 수 있는 곳이다. 일반 경기장과 같이, 불펜에는 투수의 마운드와 홈플레이트가 있다.

어휘

familiar 혤친숙한 dugout 몝더그아웃 bullpen 몝불펜 area 몝지역, 장소 side 몝측면, 옆 부분 equipment 몝장비, 기기 common 혤공통의; *흔한 warm up 준비운동을 하다 mound 몝흙무더기; *(투수의) 마운드 home plate 홈플레이트

구문 해설

4행 There is a bench inside it **for players** [*to sit on* during the game].

- for players: to sit on의 의미상 주어
- to sit on: a bench를 수식하는 형용사적 용법의 to부정사

8행 This is (the place) **where** pitchers can warm up *before entering* a game.

- where는 관계부사로, 선행사가 the place와 같이 일반적인 뜻일 경우 자주 생략됨
- before와 같은 전치사 다음에는 명사 혹은 동명사(entering)를 씀

Unit Review

A [Reading 1] infield, hitter's, pitcher's, strategies　[Reading 2] warm up

B 1 factor　2 area　3 according to　4 influence　5 fence　6 strategy

Reading 2 해석

야구에서, 각 팀에는 앉을 수 있는 더그아웃과 투수들이 경기를 위해 <u>준비운동을 할 수</u> 있는 불펜이 있다.

UNIT 09 Technology

Reading 1

[Before Reading] No, there are still some areas where machines can't replace humans.

1 ④　**2** ①　**3** patterns and style choices in Beethoven's work　**4** ②　**5** ③　**6** (1) T (2) F

해석

AI, 즉 인공지능은 정보를 가지고 업무를 수행하고 <u>스스로를 향상시키도록</u> 프로그램된 시스템이나 기계를 가리키는 단어이다. 오늘날, AI는 기술 분야에 빠른 변화를 가져올 뿐만 아니라, 예술계에서도 중요한 역할을 하고 있다.

예를 들어, 1827년 이후로 미완성으로 남아있던 루트비히 판 베토벤의 미완성 교향곡을 보아라. 베토벤의 모든 작품과 기록 외에도, AI에게는 베토벤에게 영향을 준 음악가들의 작품이 주어졌다. 마치 인간인 것처럼, AI는 그것들을 연구하여 베토벤의 작품에서 패턴과 스타일 종류를 식별할 수 있었다. 그 후, 그것은 모든 정보를 종합하여 작품을 완성했다.

또 다른 예는 <u>숨겨진</u> 파블로 피카소 그림의 발견에서 찾을 수 있다. 첨단 카메라의 도움으로, 과학자들은 '맹인의 식사' 밑에 있던 '외롭게 웅크린 누드'를 발견했다. 그 그림은 덧칠되었기 때문에, 그들은 그것을 보기 위해 엑스레이를 사용해야 했다. 그리고 나서 어려운 부분이 생겼는데, 그 그림을 재현하는 것이다. 윤곽은 이미지 처리를 통해 복원되었고 AI는 피카소가 했던 것처럼 이미지를 그리도록 훈련받았다. 가려진 채로 118년 후에, 그 그림은 3D 프린팅을 통해 되살아났다.

AI 덕분에, 우리는 <u>역사 속으로 사라졌을 수도 있었던</u> 놀라운 예술작품을 즐길 수 있다. 예술 분야에서 AI 기술의 활용은 그것(예술)의 가능성을 확실히 확장할 것이다.

어휘

artificial intelligence 인공 지능(AI)　program ⑧프로그램을 짜다[설정하다]　perform ⑧수행하다　improve ⑧향상시키다　rapid ⑧빠른　field ⑱분야　play a role 역할을 하다 (role ⑱역할)　take a look 보다　symphony ⑱교향곡　remain ⑧남다　incomplete ⑧미완성의　identify ⑧확인하다, 알아보다　complete ⑧완성하다　high-tech ⑧첨단 기술의　beneath ㉑~ 아래에　recreate ⑧되살리다, 재현하다　outline ⑱윤곽　recover ⑧되찾다; *원상복구 하다　bring ~ to life ~에 생기를 불어넣다　artwork ⑱예술작품　surely ㉑확실히　expand ⑧확장하다　[문제] imaginary ⑧상상에만 존재하는, 가상의　popularity ⑱인기　forbidden ⑧금지된　expose ⑧드러내다　animate ⑧생기를 불어넣

다; *만화로 만들다   unknown ⑱알려지지 않은

6행   For example, take a look at Ludwig van Beethoven's unfinished symphony, **which** remained incomplete since 1827.
- which: Ludwig van Beethoven's unfinished symphony를 선행사로 하는 계속적 용법의 주격 관계대명사

9행   **As if** it **were** human, the AI studied them and was able to identify patterns ...
- as if + 가정법 과거: 마치 ~인 것처럼 (현재 사실의 반대)

16행   Then came the hard part: recreating the painting.
        부사 동사   주어
- 부사 Then이 문장의 앞으로 오면서 주어와 동사가 도치됨

Reading 2   p.42

①

해석

우리는 인공지능(AI)이 어떻게 끊임없이 진화하고 점점 더 나아지고 있는지에 대해 항상 듣는다. 하지만, 어떻게 AI가 우리의 일상 생활에 실제로 더해지고 있을까? 자, AI는 특정한 목표를 달성하는 가장 좋은 방법을 알아내는 능력을 가지고 있다. AI는 엄선된 분야에서 지식을 학습하고 성장시키는 딥 러닝을 통해 이렇게 한다. 이것 때문에, AI는 우리의 요구를 만족시키기 위해 바뀔 수 있다. 기업은 AI 챗봇을 사용해 고객의 말을 번역하여 온라인으로 어떠한 고객의 질문에도 대답할 수 있다. 반면에, 병원은 환자의 데이터를 수집하고 관찰함으로써 질병을 감지하고 진단 및 치료하기 위해 AI 의사를 이용할 수 있다. 미래에, 우리는 AI가 심지어 성가신 일상 업무까지 대신하는 날을 볼 수 있을지도 모른다!

어휘

constantly ⑴끊임없이   evolve ⑧진화하다   figure out 알아내다   achieve ⑧달성하다   specific ⑱특정한   goal ⑲목표   knowledge ⑲지식   select ⑱엄선된   meet ⑧만나다; *만족시키다   need ⑲(~s) 요구   translate ⑧번역하다   detect ⑧감지하다   diagnose ⑧진단하다   treat ⑧치료하다   illness ⑲질병   take over 넘겨받다; *대신하다   annoying ⑱성가신   [문제] categorize ⑧분류하다   disaster ⑲재난, 재앙

구문 해설

3행   Well, AI has the ability [**to figure out** the best way {*to achieve* a specific goal}].
- to figure out과 to achieve는 각각 the ability와 the best way를 수식하는 형용사적 용법의 to부정사

5행   It does this through deep learning, **in which** the AI studies and grows its knowledge in select areas.
- in which 이하는 deep learning을 선행사로 하는 관계대명사절로, 선행사는 전치사 in의 목적어 역할을 함

10행   In the future, we may see the day [**when** AI even takes over annoying everyday tasks]!

• when: 선행사 the day를 수식하는 시간을 나타내는 관계부사

Unit Review   p.43

A [Reading 1] unfinished, related, beneath, recreate

B **1** role **2** select **3** popularity **4** rapid **5** achieve **6** illness

---

UNIT 10 *Teens*

Reading 1   pp.44-45

[Before Reading] I always feel stressed out when preparing for a test.

1 ③ **2** ② **3** ② **4** ① **5** ③ **6** ②

해석

케이 박사님께,

저는 학교에서 문제가 있어요. 시험을 보기 전, 제 손에서는 땀이 나고 심장이 빠르게 뛰어요. 그리고 시험 도중에는 불안해서 답을 여러 번 바꿔요. 그래서 저는 대체로 낮은 점수를 받아요. 어떻게 해야 하죠?

크리스

시험과 관련해 불안해하는 것은 정상이에요. 어느 학생에게나 한번 물어보세요! 하지만 많은 사람들은 지나치게 불안해져서 스트레스가 그들로 하여금 일을 잘 하지 못하게 할 수 있죠. 여기 시험 불안증을 줄여 줄 몇 가지 방법이 있습니다.

첫째, 약간의 스트레스는 당신에게 도움이 된다는 것을 기억하세요. 스트레스는 뭔가 중요한 일이 일어날 것이라는 당신 몸의 신호입니다. 그러므로 적극적인 접근법을 취하세요. 스트레스가 당신이 각 시험에 대비해 공부를 잘 해야 한다는 것을 생각나게 하도록 하세요. 그리고 기억하세요. 몸과 뇌는 (일을) 보다 잘 수행하기 위해 스트레스를 사용합니다. 둘째, 부정적인 생각들을 경계하세요. 부정적인 생각들은 스트레스를 증가시킬 수 있으므로 그것들을 긍정적인 생각들로 대체하세요. (답을 자주 바꾸는 것은 큰 도움이 되지 않습니다.) '나는 최선을 다할 거야!'와 '나는 열심히 공부했으니까 통과할 수 있어!' 같은 것들을 생각하려고 노력하세요. 이것은 당신이 긴장을 풀고 최선을 다하도록 도와줄 겁니다. 셋째, 과거의 실수들로부터 배우세요. 만일 지난번에 적절한 자료를 공부하지 않았거나 틀린 답을 했다면, 그 경험으로부터 배우려고 노력하세요. 과거의 실패를 미래의 성공으로 바꾸는 법을 아는 것은 아주 중요한 기술입니다! 마지막으로, 건강을 돌보세요. 연구에 의하면 충분한 수면을 취하고, 운동을 하며, 건강한 음식을 먹는 것은 스트레스를 풀어주는데, 이는 시험 성적을 향상시킬 수 있다고 합니다.

케이 박사가

어휘

sweat 몡땀 *동땀 흘리다   beat 동(심장 등이) 뛰다   nervous 형불안해하는, 초조해하는   normal 형정상적인, 보통인 reduce 동줄이다   anxiety 몡불안(증)   sign 몡신호   active 형적극적인, 의욕적인   approach *몡접근(법) 동접근하다 remind 동생각나게 하다   watch out for ~을 경계하다[조심하다]   negative 형부정적인   replace A with B A를 B로 대체하다   positive 형긍정적인   relax 동긴장을 풀다, 쉬다   material 몡자료, 재료   turn A into B A를 B로 바꿔놓다 release 동방출하다; *(긴장 등을) 풀다   performance 몡수행; *성적, 성과   [문제] get rid of ~을 제거하다   have nothing to do with ~와 아무런 관계가 없다   advice 몡조언, 충고   stay up all night 밤을 꼴딱 새우다   review 동복습하다, 검토하다   work out 운동하다

구문 해설

10행   Stress is your body's sign **that** *something important* is going to happen.

- that 이하는 your body's sign의 동격절로서 이때의 that은 '~(이)라는'의 의미임
- -thing으로 끝나는 대명사를 수식할 때는 형용사가 그 뒤에 위치함

19행   Knowing **how to turn** past failures into future successes is a valuable skill!

- Knowing ... successes는 주어로 사용된 동명사구로, 주어로 사용된 동명사구는 단수 취급함
- how to-v: ~하는 방법

Reading 2   p.46

④

해석

당신은 공부 때문에 극심한 스트레스를 느낀 적이 있는가? 뽀모도로 기법은 시간 관리의 사용을 통해 당신이 집중력을 유지하도록 도울 수 있다. 이 기법은 토마토(즉 이탈리아어로 '뽀모도로') 모양의 타이머를 사용하여 공부한 한 남자에게서 나왔다. 당신은 시간을 관리하고 집중력을 향상시키는 데 그것을 사용할 수 있다. 먼저 큰 목표들을 25분짜리 작은 과제들로 나눠라. 당신이 한 가지 과제를 일단 끝내면 짧은 휴식을 취하는데, 이것은 하나의 뽀모도로의 끝을 나타낸다. 4개의 뽀모도로를 완료한 후에는, 당신이 정보를 처리할 수 있도록 더 긴 휴식을 취해라. 지나치게 불안해하지 않고 작업을 완료하기 위해 이 기법을 사용해라. 당신은 언제든지 완료할 뽀모도로의 수를 바꿀 수 있다. 각각의 목표가 더 작은 부분으로 쪼개지면, 당신은 얼마나 많은 것을 할 수 있는지에 놀랄 것이다!

어휘

extreme 형극심한   technique 몡기법   focused 형집중한   management 몡관리 (manage 동관리하다) concentration 몡집중력   divide 동나누다   take a break 휴식을 취하다   represent 동나타내다   process 동처리하다   anxious 형긴장한, 불안해하는   [문제] break down ~을 나누다

1행   The Pomodoro technique can **help you stay** focused through the use of time management.
- help + 목적어 + (to) 동사원형: ~가 …하도록 돕다

3행   The technique came from a man [**who** used a timer {*shaped* like a tomato—or, *pomodoro* in Italian}—**to study**].
- who: 선행사 a man을 수식하는 주격 관계대명사
- shaped … Italian은 a timer를 수식하는 과거분사구
- to study: '~하기 위하여'의 의미로 목적을 나타내는 부사적 용법의 to부정사

6행   **Once** you finish a task, take a short break, *which* represents the end of one pomodoro.
- once: 일단 ~하면
- which: a short break를 선행사로 하는 계속적 용법의 주격 관계대명사

Unit Review   p.47

A   Reading 1   nervous, help, positive, mistakes, health   Reading 2   manage

B   **1** beating   **2** get rid of   **3** active   **4** approach   **5** performance   **6** relax

Reading 2 해석

뽀모도로 기법으로, 당신은 일을 더 작은 부분으로 나누고 각각의 일 사이에 휴식을 취함으로써 시간을 관리할 수 있다.

Before Reading I've read some articles about people who had to move from their home because of climate change.

1 ④   **2** ②   **3** ④   **4** It could sink into the sea.   **5** ④   **6** (1) T (2) F

해석

기후 변화는 아마도 세계의 최대 문제일 것이다. 많은 사람들은 이미 이것을 알고 있다. 그러나 대부분의 사람들이 기후 변화가 이미 사람들의 삶을 해치고 있다는 것은 모른다. '기후 난민'이 세계 여러 곳에서 생겨나고 있다. 이들은 기후 변화 때문에 자신의 조국을 잃어버린 사람들이다.

사실, 대부분의 이런 문제들은 선진국에서 생기는 오염으로 인해 발생한다. 가난한 나라들은 우리 세계에 영향을 미치고 있는 기후 변화에 책임이 없다. 그러나 슬프게도, 거의 모든 기후 난민은 가난한 나라들에서 생긴다. 여기에는 태평양에 있는 투발루 같은 나라들이 포함된다. 기후 변화로 인해, 투발루 주변의 해수면은 지난 23년간 매년 1.2밀리미터씩 상승해 왔다. 과학자들은 21세기 말이면 투발루가 바닷속으로 가라앉을 수도 있다고 염려하고 있다. 해수면 상승과 더불어, 기후 변화는 위험한 폭풍우를 만들어낸다. 방글라데시의 많은 사람들은 폭풍우를 피하기 위해 기후 난민으로서 인도로 이주했다.

기후 난민은 여러 가지 문제들에 직면한다. 집을 떠나왔기 때문에, 그들은 살 곳도 없고 직업도 없다. 게다가 그들은 많은 나라에서 환영받지 못한다. 어떤 나라들은 난민들을 도우려고 노력하고, 기후 변화를 멈추기 위해 힘쓰고 있다. 그러나 이것은 충분하지 않다. 전 세계가 이 문제를 해결하기 위해서 함께 노력할 필요가 있다.

어휘

climate change 기후 변화 (climate 몡기후)   refugee 몡피난자, 난민   homeland 몡고국, 모국   cause 몡원인 *동야기하다, 일으키다   pollution 몡오염   developed country 선진국   responsible 혱책임이 있는   affect 동영향을 미치다   include 동포함하다   sea level 해수면   sink 동가라앉다   in addition to ~와 더불어   storm 몡폭풍우   escape 동도망치다, 피하다   face 몡얼굴 *동직면하다   solve 동해결하다   [문제] harm 몡해, 피해 *동해치다   give up on ~에 대해 포기하다   take responsibility for ~에 대해 책임을 지다

구문 해설

7행   Poor countries aren't responsible for the climate change [**that**'s affecting our world].

• that: 선행사 the climate change를 수식하는 주격 관계대명사

14행   Many people in Bangladesh **have moved** to India *as* climate refugees to escape the storms.

• have moved: 결과를 나타내는 현재완료

• as: (역할·자격) ~로서

16행   (Being) Away from home, they have no place [**to live**] and no jobs.

- Away from home은 앞에 being이 생략된 분사구문으로, 이유를 나타냄 (← As they are away from home)
- to live: no place를 수식하는 형용사적 용법의 to부정사

Reading 2   p.50

③

해석

투발루의 미래를 구하기 위한 호소

2021년 11월 5일, 투발루의 장관 사이먼 코페는 유엔이 기후 변화에 신속히 대응할 것을 촉구했다. 그의 목표는 해수면 상승이 섬나라에 미치는 영향들에 대한 인식을 높이는 것이었다. 언제나 그랬듯이, 코페는 연설을 할 때 양복과 넥타이를 매고 있었다. 그러나 육지 대신, 그는 물에 무릎까지 잠긴 채 서 있었다. 섬의 다른 많은 지역들처럼, 그 지역은 과거에는 육지였다. "기후 변화는 우리를 기다리지 않을 것입니다"라고 그가 말했다. 투발루와 같은 저지대 섬들은 바다로 가라앉고 있고, 그것은 사람들을 걱정시키고 있다. 장관은 "그 섬들은 우리 조상들의 고향이었고, 오늘날 우리 민족의 고향이며, 우리는 그 섬들이 미래에도 우리 민족의 고향으로 남아 있기를 바랍니다"라며 그의 섬을 위해 호소했다. 투발루인들은 아무것도 바뀌지 않는다면 그들의 고향을 떠나야 할지도 모른다고 두려워한다.

어휘

call 똉요청, 요구   minister 똉장관   urge 똉촉구하다   raise 똉불러일으키다   awareness 똉인식   nation 똉국가   deliver 똉배달하다; *(연설·강연 등을) 하다   speech 똉연설   knee-deep 똉무릎까지 올라오는, 무릎까지 잠긴   low-lying 똉낮은, 저지대의   plead 똉애원하다   ancestor 똉조상   [문제] issue 똉문제   unsolved 똉해결되지 않은   take action 조치를 취하다, 행동에 옮기다   immediate 똉즉각적인

구문 해설

3행   His goal was **to raise** awareness about the effects of rising sea levels on the island nation.
- to raise: '~하는 것'의 의미로 보어로 사용된 명사적 용법의 to부정사

8행   Like many other parts of the island, the area **used to be** land.
- used to-v: ~하곤 했다, (과거에는) ~이었다 (과거의 습관이나 상태를 표현)

11행   Low-lying islands like Tuvalu are sinking into the ocean, **which** worries the people.
                주어   동사
- which: 앞 절 내용 전체(Low-lying islands ... the ocean)를 선행사로 하는 계속적 용법의 주격 관계대명사

Unit Review   p.51

A   Reading 1   homelands, poor, storms, developed   Reading 2   sink

B   1 escape   2 solve   3 refugee   4 ancestor   5 climate   6 urge

Reading 1 해석

우리 지구의 변화하는 기후는 많은 문제들을 일으키고 있다. 기후 변화 때문에 그들의 조국을 떠나야만 하는 사람들은 '기후 난민'으로 알려져 있다. 이 사람들의 대부분은 가난한 나라 출신이다. 예를 들어, 투발루 섬은 바다로 가라앉을 수 있고, 방글라데시는 극심한 폭풍우를 겪고 있다. 하지만, 기후 변화의 주된 원인은 바로 선진국들에서 발생한 오염이다. 이 국가들은 기후 난민을 돕고 기후 변화를 막기 위해 노력해야 한다.

Reading 2 해석

투발루의 장관 사이먼 코페는 유엔이 기후 변화에 신속히 대응할 것을 촉구했는데, 기후 변화가 저지대 섬들을 바닷속으로 가라앉도록 유발하고 있기 때문이다.

UNIT 12 Literature

Reading 1
pp.52-53

Before Reading If I could find something to eat and some water, maybe I would survive for a few days.

1 ③ **2** He shot his gun straight into the air. **3** ④ **4** ③ **5** ② **6** (1) F (2) T

해석

로빈슨 크루소는 영국인 선원이었다. 여정 중 폭풍우가 그의 배를 부숴버렸고, 그는 어느 섬에 남겨졌다. 그는 자신이 그곳에 살고 있는 유일한 존재라고 생각했지만…

식인종들은 그들의 저녁 만찬을 준비하느라 바빴다. 그들은 그들의 죄수를 보고 있지 않았다. 나는 그가 몰래 그의 밧줄을 푸는 것을 보았다. 그러고 나서 그는 갑자기 뛰어올라 재빨리 개울을 향해 뛰기 시작했다. 식인종 세 명이 화가 나서 소리치며 그를 뒤쫓았다. 나는 그를 돕고 싶어서, 바위 뒤에서 뛰어나왔다. 나는 공중에 대고 똑바로 총을 쐈다. 빵! 식인종들은 내 총소리에 너무 깜짝 놀라 도망쳤다.

불쌍한 죄수는 가까이에 서 있었다. 그는 추웠고, 젖어 있었으며, 매우 겁에 질려 있었다. 나는 그의 이름을 몰랐기에, 그를 프라이데이라고 불렀다. 그날이 금요일이었고, 나는 더 나은 이름을 생각해낼 수 없었다. 나는 그에게 상냥하게 말했고, 많이 미소 지었다. 그는 내 말을 알아듣지 못했지만, 내가 친절하다는 것을 알 수 있었다. 그는 더 가까이 다가왔고 그의 손을 위아래로 움직이기 시작했다. 나는 그가 자신의 목숨을 구해줘서 내게 고마워하고 있다는 것을 알 수 있었다.

나는 그를 언덕 위 내 집으로 데려갔다. 그에게 앉으라고 청하고 빵과 치즈 등 약간의 음식을 주었다. 내가 다른 누군가와 함께 식사를 한 마지막 때가 언제였던가? 확실히 20년 이상은 되었다! 식사를 마치자, 프라이데이는 바닥에서 빠르게 잠이 들었다.

어휘

sailor 몡 선원   destroy 툉 파괴하다   prepare for ~을 준비하다   untie 툉 풀다   suddenly 囝 갑자기   stream 몡 시내, 개울   chase 툉 뒤쫓다   shout 툉 소리지르다   shoot 툉 (총·화살 등을) 쏘다   straight 囝 똑바로   frightened 휑 깜짝

놀란, 겁에 질린 run away 도망치다 nearby 튀 가까이에 gently 튀 상냥하게 tell 동 말하다; *알다, 판단하다 save 동 저축하다; 절약하다; *구하다 lead 동 이끌다, 인도하다 share 동 공유하다, 나누다 [문제] enemy 명 적 pirate 명 해적 relieved 형 안심한 disappointed 형 실망한 alone 형 혼자, 외로운

구문 해설

5행 I **watched him** secretly **untie** his ropes.
- 지각동사(watch) + 목적어 + 동사원형: ~가 …하는 것을 보다

9행 The cannibals were **so frightened** by the noise of my gun **that** they ran away.
- so + 형용사/부사 + that …: 너무 ~해서 …하다

17행 When was the last time [**that** I had shared a meal with someone else]?
- that: 시간을 나타내는 관계부사, 선행사에 최상급의 의미가 있을 경우 when 대신 that이 사용됨

Reading 2 p.54

③

해석

'로빈슨 크루소'는 영국 작가 대니얼 디포에 의해 1719년에 쓰인 소설이다. 그것은 매우 유명한 소설로, 거의 300년 동안 독자들의 인기를 얻어왔다. 그러나 로빈슨 크루소의 이야기가 사실은 실화에 바탕을 둔 것이라는 것을 아는 사람은 거의 없다. 1704년에 대니얼 디포는 알렉산더 셀커크라고 하는 스코틀랜드 선원에 관해 들었다. 그는 배의 선장과 다투었고 칠레 부근 작은 섬에 남겨졌다. 그는 구조되기 전 4년간 그곳에 홀로 머물렀다. 셀커크의 경험에 관해 듣고 난 후, 디포는 '로빈슨 크루소'를 썼다. 흥미롭게도, 1966년, 많은 사랑을 받은 소설 속 등장인물을 기념하여 그 섬의 이름은 '로빈슨 크루소 섬'으로 변경되었다.

어휘

novel 명 소설 captain 명 선장 rescue 동 구조하다 in honor of ~을 기념하여 character 명 성격; *(소설 등의) 등장인물 [문제] inspire 동 영감을 주다 legend 명 전설 be based on ~에 근거하다

구문 해설

9행 … the name of the island **was changed to** "Robinson Crusoe Island" in honor of …
　　　　　　　　　　　　A　　　　　　　　　　　　　　　　　B
- A is changed to B: 'A가 B로 바뀌다'라는 의미로 'change A to B' 구문이 수동태로 사용된 형태

Unit Review p.55

A [Reading 1] escaped, gun, friendly, share [Reading 2] alone

B 1 share 2 chasing 3 untie 4 in honor of 5 is based on 6 destroyed

27

로빈슨 크루소는 몇몇 식인종들이 한 죄수를 먹으려고 준비하고 있을 때 지켜보고 있었다. 하지만 그때 그 죄수는 밧줄에서 <u>탈출해</u> 달리기 시작했다. 크루소는 숨어있던 곳에서 뛰어나와 하늘을 향해 총을 쏘았다. 시끄러운 소리는 식인종들이 도망치게 만들었다. 크루소는 그 남자에게 자신이 <u>친절하다는</u> 것을 보여주기 위해 미소를 지었다. 그는 그 남자를 프라이데이라고 부르기로 했다. 크루소는 프라이데이를 집으로 데려가서 그에게 먹을 것을 주었으며, 수년 만에 누군가와 식사를 <u>함께 하는</u> 것을 기뻐했다. 금세, 프라이데이는 잠이 들었다.

대니얼 디포는 섬에 4년 동안 <u>혼자</u> 있었던 스코틀랜드 선원에 대한 이야기를 듣고 '로빈슨 크루소'를 썼다.

UNIT 13 Science

Reading 1

pp.56-57

Before Reading Well, if the painting was made with perfumed colors, we could smell the painting while looking at it.

1 ②　**2** who have a special sense known as synesthesia　**3** ②　**4** ④　**5** ②　**6** ④

해석

숫자 4는 무슨 색인가? 5월은 슬픈가 아니면 행복한가? 대부분의 사람들에게 이런 질문들은 허튼소리이다. 그러나 공감각이라고 알려진 특별한 감각을 가진 사람들에게 그것들은 전혀 이상하지 않다. 공감각은 사람들이 어떤 것들에 관해 느끼고 생각하는 방식에 영향을 미친다. 그것은 시각 같은 한 가지 감각과 청각 같은 또 다른 감각이 혼합된 것이다.

보고된 공감각에는 60개 이상의 각기 다른 유형이 있다. 예를 들어, 어떤 사람들은 그들이 특정한 문자나 숫자를 볼 때 자동으로 어떤 색깔을 떠올린다. 다른 사람들은 장미 향기를 맡을 때마다 특정한 소리를 듣기도 한다. 공감각을 가진 유명한 사람들이 여럿 있었다. 그들 중 한 명은 러시아 화가인 Wassily Kandinsky였다. 그는 <u>시각과 청각</u>이 혼합된 감각을 경험했다. 그림을 그릴 때, 그는 각각의 색깔이 만들어내는 음악이 들렸다.

우리가 공감각에 관해 많이 알고 있다는 사실에도 불구하고, 과학자들은 무엇이 그것을 야기하는지 여전히 정확히 알지 못한다. 그들은 두뇌 안에서 어떤 혼동이 있다고 생각한다. 한 감각에 속해야 하는 두뇌의 일부분이 다른 감각에 의해 사용되는 것이다. <u>두뇌의 서로 다른 부분 사이의 이러한 '연결'은 아마도 태어날 때 만들어질 것이다.</u> 사실, 어떤 과학자들은 많은 어린이들이 공감각을 가지고 있다고 생각한다. 그들이 나이가 들면서, 그들 두뇌의 이상한 연결이 사라지는 것이다.

어휘

nonsense 명 허튼소리　sense 명 감각 동 느끼다　synesthesia 명 공감각　mixing 명 혼합 (mix 동 혼합하다)　sight 명 시각, 시력　report 동 보고하다　automatically 부 자동적으로　despite 전 ~에도 불구하고　confusion 명 혼동, 착각　be supposed to ~하기로 되어 있다　belong to ~에 속하다　connection 명 연결　disappear 동 사라지다　[문제]

creative 휑창의적인　unique 휑독특한　birth 똉탄생, 출생　so far 지금까지　memorize 동암기하다

2행　　But to **those** [**who** have a special sense {(which *is*) *known as* synesthesia}], ...

- who: those를 수식하는 주격 관계대명사로, those who는 '~하는 사람들'이라는 의미
- be known as: ~라고 알려지다

10행　　Others may hear a certain sound **every time** they smell a rose.

- every time: '(~할) 때마다'의 의미로 절을 연결하는 접속사처럼 쓰임

14행　　Despite the fact **that** we know a lot about synesthesia, scientists still don't know exactly

what causes it.

- that: 동격절을 이끄는 접속사로 '~라는'의 의미
- what causes it은 know의 목적어 역할을 하는 간접의문문

Reading 2　　　　　　　　　　　　　　　　　　　　　　　　　　　　　p.58

③

해석

당신은 시 수업에서 공감각이 언급되는 것을 들었을 것이다. 그것은 '공감각'이라는 용어가 시인이 감각들 간의 연결을 표현할 때 사용되기 때문이다. 예를 들어, 시인은 '단단한 금속성의 소리'나 '맛있는 느낌'에 관해 이야기할 수 있을 것이다. 사실, 공감각은 영어에서 흔하다. 공감각은 또한 음악에서도 언급되는데, 사람들은 음조를 특정한 색깔과 연결시키는 경향이 있기 때문이다. 일반적으로 사람들은 높은 음을 밝은색과, 낮은 음을 어두운색과 연결시킨다. 실제의 공감각은 아주 흔하지 않지만, 사람들은 그것을 쉽게 이해할 수 있는 것 같다. 그러니, '비단결 같은 목소리'나 '짙고 붉은 소리'를 상상하려고 노력해보아라. 당신은 그것이 쉽다는 것을 발견할 것이다.

어휘

mention 동언급하다　poetry 똉(문학) 시 (poet 똉시인)　term 똉*용어; 학기, 기간　metallic 휑금속성의　tend to-v ~하는 경향이 있다　connect 동연결하다, 관련지어 생각하다　tone 똉음조, 음색　particular 휑*특정한; 특별한　silky 휑부드러운, 비단 같은　[문제] in general 일반적으로　light 휑*밝은; 가벼운

구문 해설

1행　　You might **hear synesthesia mentioned** in a poetry class.

- 지각동사(hear) + 목적어 + 목적보어: 목적어와 목적보어의 관계가 수동이므로 목적보어로 과거분사를 씀

Unit Review

A Reading 1 mixed, types, wrong, birth Reading 2 connection

B **1** sight **2** confusion **3** silky **4** mention **5** term **6** sense

Reading 2 해석

공감각은 서로 다른 감각들을 연결하기 위해 영어 및 음악에서 종종 사용된다.

UNIT 14 *The Economy*

Reading 1

Before Reading I check the brand and its price first, as I care about brand names a lot.

1 ② **2** ③ **3** ① **4** ③ **5** ③ **6** (1) F (2) F

해석

쇼핑은 어려울 수 있다. 선택할 수 있는 제품들이 너무 많이 있다! 그래서 마케팅 담당자들은 고객들이 그들의 제품을 선택하게 만들기 위해 특별한 기법들을 사용한다. 이 기법들 중 하나는 '헝거(hunger) 마케팅 전략'으로 알려져 있다.

먼저, 매력적인 신제품이 출시된다. 그다음에, 회사는 소량의 제품만을 판매한다. 이것은 그 제품이 모두에게 충분하지 않은 것처럼 보이게 만드는데, 왜냐하면 그 제품에 대한 수요가 공급보다 훨씬 더 높기 때문이다. 나중에, 그 회사는 그 제품을 대량으로 판매하고 큰 수익을 낸다. 헝거 마케팅은 또한 회사의 브랜드 이미지에 도움이 된다. 많은 사람들이 그들이 쉽게 얻을 수 없는 것을 원할 때, 그 제품에 대한 여론은 상승한다.

애플은 이 기법을 성공적으로 활용하는 회사이다. 그들이 신제품을 만들 때마다, 그것을 구매하기 위해 기다리는 사람들이 길게 줄 서 있다. (애플의 첫 번째 제품은 '애플 컴퓨터 I'이었다.) 그것은 그 회사가 공급량을 신중하게 제한하고 그것(공급량)을 낮은 상태로 유지하기 때문이다. 그 결과, 애플은 인기 있는 브랜드 이미지를 계속 가질 수 있다. 중국의 스마트폰 제조사인 샤오미는 약간 다른 방식으로 헝거 마케팅을 이용한다. 그들은 그들의 제품을 구하기 어렵게 만들 뿐만 아니라, 또한 가격을 매우 낮게 설정한다.

그러니 다음에 여러분이 신제품을 사려고 줄을 서서 기다리고 있을 때, 스스로 이 질문을 해보아라. 이 제품이 정말 구하기 어려운가? 아니면 이것은 단지 헝거 마케팅의 또 다른 사례인가?

어휘

product 명상품 choose 동선택하다 marketer 명마케팅 담당자 customer 명손님, 고객 hunger 명배고픔; 갈구
strategy 명계획, 전략 attractive 형매력적인 introduce 동소개하다; *(상품 등을) 내놓다 demand 명요구; *수요
supply 명공급(량) profit 명이익, 수익 (profitable 형수익성 있는) opinion 명의견; 여론 successfully 부성공적으로
carefully 부주의하여, 신중하게 control 동지배하다; *제한하다 manufacturer 명제조자, 제조사 slightly 부약간, 조금

[문제] competition ⑱ 경쟁   high-tech ⑲ 첨단 기술의

6행　This **makes *it* seem** like there isn't enough for everyone, ... is <u>much</u> higher than the supply.

- 사역동사(make) + 목적어 + 동사원형: ~가 …하게 하다
- it은 앞 문장의 the product를 가리킴
- much: even, a lot 등과 함께 비교급을 강조하는 말로 '훨씬'의 의미

14행　..., there are long lines of <u>people</u> [(who are) waiting **to buy** it].

- people과 waiting 사이에는 '주격 관계대명사 + be동사'가 생략되어 있음
- to buy: '~하기 위하여'의 의미로 쓰인 부사적 용법의 to부정사

18행　**Not only** <u>do they make</u> their products hard to get, **but** they **also** set their prices very low.
　　　　　조동사 주어 동사

- not only A but also B: A뿐만 아니라 B도
- 부정어(not only)가 문장 앞에 오면서 주어와 동사가 도치되었으며, 일반동사의 경우 조동사 do를 사용하여 도치함

Reading 2　　　　　　　　　　　　　　　　　　　　　　　　　p.62

③

해석

　당신이 재미로 온라인 상점을 방문하는데, 갑자기 '당신은 방금 그것을 놓쳤어요! 우리의 최신 키보드는 어제 매진되었습니다.'라고 하는 광고가 나타난다고 해보자. **(B)** 당신은 기회를 놓쳤다고 생각하면서, 다시 거래를 놓치지 않도록 다른 키보드를 구입한다. 축하한다, 당신은 방금 FOMO 마케팅에 빠진 것이다. **(C)** FOMO는 다른 사람들이 가지고 있는 것에 대한 '놓칠 것에 대한 두려움(fear of missing out)'이다. 당신은 다른 사람들이 당신이 가지고 있지 않은 어떤 것을 가지고 있을 때 그들이 더 나은 삶을 살고 있다고 느낄 수 있다. 그래서 이 기법을 사용함으로써, 마케팅 담당자들은 고객들이 무분별하고 불필요한 구매를 하도록 이끈다. **(A)** 그들이 당신을 속이지 못하게 해라. 다른 사람들이 가지고 있는 것과 당신이 부족한 것에 항상 초점을 맞추는 것은 엄청나게 스트레스를 줄 수 있다. 인생에서 당신이 놓치는 것에 초점을 맞추기보다는, 당신이 정말로 필요로 하는 것에 초점을 맞추도록 해보아라. 그러면 당신은 더 현명하게 소비할 수 있다.

어휘

for fun 재미로   advertisement ⑲ 광고   appear ⑧ 나타나다   miss ⑧ *놓치다; 그리워하다   sell out 다 팔리다, 매진되다   fool ⑧ 속이다, 기만하다   focus on ~에 초점을 맞추다   lack ⑧ 부족하다   incredibly ⑨ 믿을 수 없을 정도로, 엄청나게   wisely ⑨ 현명하게   opportunity ⑲ 기회   deal ⑲ 거래, 합의   thoughtless ⑲ 생각 없는, 무분별한   unnecessary ⑲ 불필요한   purchase ⑲ 구매

31

1행   ..., and suddenly <u>an advertisement</u> appears [**that** says "You just missed it! ...]

- that: 선행사 an advertisement를 수식하는 주격 관계대명사

4행   <u>Always focusing on [**what** others have] and [**what** you are lacking]</u> <u>can be</u> incredibly stressful.

- what: 선행사를 포함하는 관계대명사로 '~하는 것'의 의미

8행   **Thinking** (that) **you've missed an opportunity**, you buy another keyboard to avoid losing out on a deal again.

- Thinking ... opportunity는 동시동작을 나타내는 분사구문으로 '~하면서'의 의미
- Thinking 뒤에는 명사절을 이끄는 접속사 that이 생략되어 있음

Unit Review   p.63

A   Reading 1   introduced, small, demand, large   Reading 2   missing out

B   **1** opinion   **2** control   **3** purchase   **4** focus on   **5** appear   **6** fool

---

Reading 2 해석

고객들은 물건에 대한 '놓칠 것에 대한 두려움' 때문에 불필요한 구매를 한다.

UNIT 15 *Health*

Reading 1   pp.64-65

Before Reading   I think they are better than eating fast food or other unhealthy snacks.

1 ①   **2** ④   **3** give us more energy and can even help us think better   **4** ②   **5** ③   **6** ③

해석

잭은 건강을 위해 매일 에너지 바 몇 개를 먹는다. 샐리는 살을 빼기 위해 에너지 바를 먹는다. 그들은 건강에 좋은 선택을 하고 있다, 그렇지 않은가? 어떤 사람들은 그렇다고 생각할지도 모르지만, 잭과 샐리는 <u>에너지 바가 그들이 생각하는 것만큼 좋지 않을 수 있다는 것을 알아야</u> 한다.

광고는 우리에게 이런 에너지 바가 더 많은 에너지를 주고, 심지어는 더 잘 생각하도록 도와줄 수 있다고 말한다. 이 때문에 많은 사람들은 에너지 바를 건강식품 중 한 종류라고 느낀다. 그러나 대부분의 에너지 바는 사실 설탕, 카페인, 또는 지방으로 가득 차 있다. 그

래서 그것을 너무 많이 먹는 것은 당신의 건강에 해로울 수 있다. 이것은 특히 하루에 두 개 이상의 바를 먹거나 규칙적인 식사 대신 바를 먹는 사람들에게 그러하다. 에너지 바가 감자칩, 사탕, 그리고 다른 정크 푸드보다 더 영양가 있을 수는 있지만, 그것들은 제대로 된 식사만큼 건강에 좋지는 않다.

　에너지 바는 또한 높은 열량을 포함하고 있다. 많은 바들이 운동선수들에게 에너지를 주기 위해 높은 열량으로 만들어진다. (몇몇 고칼로리 음식들은 에너지를 제공하지만 맛있지 않다.) 그러나, 보통 사람들이 이런 바를 규칙적으로 먹으면, 너무 많은 열량을 섭취하게 된다. 이것은 체중 증가나 다른 건강 문제들을 일으킬 수 있다.

　가끔 에너지 바를 먹는 것은 빠른 식사를 해야 하는 사람들이나 육체적인 활동을 준비하는 사람들에게 도움이 될 수 있다. 그러나 너무 많이 먹는 것은 전혀 먹지 않는 것보다 더 해로울 수 있다.

어휘

lose weight 살이 빠지다 (weight 몡체중)　commercial *몡상업 광고 몡상업의　caffeine 몡카페인　fat 몡지방
regular 몡*규칙적인; 일상의 (regularly 부규칙적으로)　nutritious 몡영양가 있는　contain 동포함하다　calorie 몡열량
count 몡*총수, 총계 동세다　athlete 몡운동선수　ordinary 몡평범한, 보통의　gain 몡증가 동획득하다; 증가하다
occasional 몡이따금의, 가끔의　physical 몡신체적인　activity 몡활동　[문제] benefit 몡이익, 이득　source 몡근본,
원인; *원천　value 몡가치　bitter 몡(맛이) 쓴　venture 동과감히 ~하다

구문 해설

5행　Commercials tell us that these bars ... and can even **help us think** better.
　　　동사　간접목적어　　　　　　　　　　직접목적어
　　　• help + 목적어 + (to) 동사원형: ~가 …하도록 돕다

10행　This is especially true for people **who**　┌ eat more than two bars a day
　　　　　　　　　　　　　　　　　　　　　　　│ or
　　　　　　　　　　　　　　　　　　　　　　　└ eat them instead of a regular meal.
　　　• who: people을 수식하는 주격 관계대명사

11행　While energy bars ..., they are **not as healthy as** a full meal.
　　　• not as + 형용사/부사 + as ...: …만큼 ~하지 않은

Reading 2　　　　　　　　　　　　　　　　　　　　　　　　　　　　　　p.66

④

영양성분	
1회 분량 1컵 (230g)	
용기당 총 분량 2컵	
1회 분량당 함량	
열량 80	
	% 영양소 기준치
총 지방 0.5g	1%
포화지방 0g	0%
트랜스지방 0g	0%
콜레스테롤 0g	0%
나트륨 960mg	40%
총 탄수화물 17g	6%
식이섬유 2g	
당류 4g	
단백질 4g 미만	
비타민 A 10%	비타민 C 0%
칼슘 4%	철분 4%

영양성분 함량표 이해하기: 야채 수프 한 캔

영양성분 함량표는 사람들이 자신이 먹는 음식에 무엇이 들어 있는지 이해하도록 돕는다. 여기 야채 수프 한 캔에 대한 영양성분 함량표가 있다. '1회 분량'은 보통 한 끼에 섭취되는 제품의 양을 나타낸다. 이 표에서는 수프 1회분이 한 컵과 동일하고, 이는 230g이다. '용기당 총 분량'은 이 캔에 몇 회 분량이 들어 있는지를 나타낸다. 만약 이 수프 한 캔 전체를 먹으면, 당신은 2회 분량을 먹게 된다. 그것은 표에 있는 열량과 영양분의 두 배이다. '열량'은 전체 용기당이 아닌, 1회 분량당 열량을 나타낸다. 따라서 저열량 식품을 사고 싶다면 반드시 열량과 1회 분량을 모두 확인하도록 하라. 이 수프는 전체 용기에 2컵 분량이 들어있고, 전체 용기에 대한 칼로리는 80 (→ 160)이다. '% 영양소 기준치'는 하루 2,000 칼로리 식단에 근거하여 주요 영양소들이 각 회 분량에 얼마나 포함되어 있는지를 보여준다. 1회 분량이 어떤 영양소를 5% 미만 함유하고 있다면 그것은 소량으로 여겨진다. 그리고 20% 이상이 있다면, 그것은 많은 것이다. 표에 따르면, 이 수프는 너무 많은 나트륨을 포함하고 있다.

nutrition 몡영양(물)　label 몡표, 라벨　serving 몡한 끼분의 음식　amount 몡양, 분량　normally 뿐보통, 통상적으로　equal 혱똑같은 *동~와 같다　container 몡용기, 그릇　double 혱두 배의 *동~을 두 배로 하다　nutrient 몡영양분, 영양소　daily 혱매일의　consider 동고려하다; *여기다　sodium 몡나트륨　[표] saturated fat 포화지방　trans fat 트랜스지방　cholesterol 몡콜레스테롤　carbohydrate 몡탄수화물　dietary fiber 식이섬유　protein 몡단백질　iron 몡철, 쇠; *철분

3행　"Serving Size" shows the amount of the product [(which is) normally eaten in one meal].

• the product 뒤에는 '주격 관계대명사 + be동사'가 생략되어 있음

10행 So, if you want ..., **be sure to check** *both* the calories *and* the serving size.

- be sure to-v: 확실히 ∼하다
- both A and B: A와 B 둘 다

Unit Review
p.67

A [Reading 1] Commercials, harmful, regular, calories, fast

B **1** activity **2** athlete **3** daily **4** occasional **5** physical **6** serving

---

UNIT 16 *Culture*

Reading 1
pp.68-69

[Before Reading] No, I've never heard such a name.

1 ③ **2** it is actually a dried-up river that usually has no water in it **3** ② **4** ③ **5** ④
6 ②

해석

헨리-온-토드 레가타(Henley-on-Todd Regatta)는 호주의 앨리스 스프링스에 있는 토드 강에서 매년 열리는 '보트' 경주이다. 이 보트 경주는 독특한데, 토드 강이 사실은 대개 물이 없는 바싹 마른 강이기 때문이다.

그것은 자선 목적으로 돈을 모으고자 했던 한 지역 사람에 의해 1962년에 시작되었다. 그는 유명한 헨리-온-템스 레가타(Henley-on-Thames Regatta)에서 아이디어를 얻었다. 그것은 잉글랜드에서 매년 열리는 보트 경주이다. 그가 바랐던 것처럼 토드 강의 뜨겁고 깊은 모래에서 열린 보트 경주는 매우 재미있었다. 수년 동안, 헨리-온-토드 레가타는 축제와 우스운 경주의 날이 되었다.

주 경기에서, 팀들은 뜨겁고 건조한 모래 사이로 달려야 한다. '보트'에는 밑바닥이 없기 때문에, 팀들은 달리는 동안 그것들을 붙잡고 있어야 한다! 모든 사람들은 팀들이 결승선에 도착하기 위해 애쓰는 동안 웃고 환호한다. 그 후에는, 노 대신 모래삽이 사용되는 카누 경기가 있다. 마지막 행사는 인기 있는 전함 대결이다. 전함처럼 꾸며진 트럭들이 모래를 따라 경주하고 팀들은 밀가루 폭탄과 물대포를 가지고 싸운다!

매우 재미있기 때문에, 그 경주는 매년 많은 군중을 불러 모은다. 가장 좋은 점은, 시작된 이래로 그것은 전 세계 수많은 자선단체들을 위해 백만 달러 이상을 모금해왔다는 것이다.

어휘

regatta 명보트[요트] 경주   dried-up 형바싹 마른   local 형지방의, 지역의   raise 동올리다; *모으다   charity 명자선(단체)
entertaining 형재미있는   celebration 명축하, 축제   silly 형바보 같은   main 형주요한   bottom 명밑바닥   cheer
동환호하다, 응원하다   finish line 결승선   afterwards 부뒤에, 나중에   shovel 명삽   oar 명노   battleship 명전함
decorate 동장식하다   flour 명밀가루   bomb 명폭탄   cannon 명대포   draw 동당기다; *끌다, 매혹하다   crowd 명

군중 [문제] forward ⓤ 앞으로 strengthen ⓥ 강화하다

7행 As he **had hoped**, the boat race, (which was) held in the hot ..., was very entertaining.
- had hoped: 주절 동사의 시제인 과거(was)보다 앞선 때의 일을 나타내는 과거완료
- held 앞에는 '주격 관계대명사 + be동사'가 생략되어 있음

18행 **Being highly entertaining**, the race draws large crowds every year.
- Being highly entertaining: 문맥상 '이유'를 나타내는 분사구문
  (= As it is highly entertaining)

Reading 2   p.70

①

해석

헨리-온-템스 레가타는 잉글랜드의 템스 강에서 매년 7월에 열리는 조정 경기이다. 그것은 1839년에 처음 열렸고, 단 하루 동안만 했다. 지금 그것은 5일 동안 계속되고, 전 세계에서 온 조정 팀들이 참가한다. 이 행사는 아주 인기가 많아서 팀들은 대회 참가 자격을 얻기 위해 미리 경쟁해야 한다. 보트 경주 기간 중 매일, 각각의 경주에 단 2개의 보트가 경쟁하는 경기가 100개에 이른다. 그러나 보트 경주는 볼거리의 절반일 뿐이다! 보트 경주는 영국 왕실 가족들을 포함한 부유하고, 중요한 인물들을 불러들이는 것으로도 유명하다. 그래서 많은 사람들이 군중 속에서 왕자나 공주를 보길 바라면서 그 행사를 찾는다!

어휘

rowing ⓝ 배젓기; *조정 last ⓥ 지속하다 compete ⓥ 경쟁하다 (competition ⓝ 경쟁; *경기, 대회) beforehand ⓤ 이전에, 미리 place ⓝ 장소; *(선수로서의) 자격 up to ~에 이르는 attraction ⓝ 매력적인 것, 볼거리 (attract ⓥ (흥미를) 끌다, 매혹하다) royal ⓐ 왕[여왕]의, 왕실의

구문 해설

4행 The event is **so popular that** teams must compete beforehand *to win* a place in the competition.
- so + 형용사/부사 + that ...: 너무 ~해서 (그 결과) …하다
- to win: '~하기 위해서'라는 의미로 목적을 나타내는 부사적 용법의 to부정사

8행 Thus, many people visit the event **hoping** to see a prince or princess in the crowd!
- hoping 이하는 '~하면서'라는 뜻의 동시동작을 나타내는 분사구문

A   Reading 1   dried-up, charity, bottomless, shovels, fun   Reading 2   rowing

B   **1** cheered   **2** raised   **3** decorated   **4** up to   **5** main   **6** competition

---

Reading 1 해석

매년, 호주의 앨리스 스프링스 도시는 헨리-온-토드 레가타를 개최한다. 그것은 바싹 마른 강에서 하는 보트 경주이다. 그것은 자선기금을 모으기 위해 1962년에 시작되었다. 팀들은 달릴 때 바닥이 없는 보트를 들고서, 모래 사이로 경주를 한다. 또한 노 대신에 삽을 사용하는 카누 경기도 있다. 마지막 행사는 전함 대결이다. 전함처럼 꾸며진 트럭들은 위에 탄 사람들이 물과 밀가루로 싸우는 동안 경주를 한다. 그것은 매우 재미있는 행사이고, 그것은 많은 자선기금을 모은다.

Reading 2 해석

헨리-온-템스 레가타에서 사람들은 조정 팀들이 경기에서 경주하는 것을 관람할 수 있고 심지어 영국 왕실 가족도 볼 수 있을 지도 모른다.

UNIT 17   *Issues*

Reading 1   pp.72-73

Before Reading   I found an unknown SNS user who took my selfies without any permission and posted my pictures online as if they were hers.

1 ①   **2** ②   **3** ①   **4** ②   **5** ③   **6** (1) F   (2) T

해석

당신이 만약 대부분의 십대와 같다면, 당신은 아마도 다양한 소셜 네트워크 서비스(SNS)를 이용할 것이다. 이런 서비스들은 당신이 프로필을 만들고, 당신에 관한 정보를 게시하고, 당신의 친구들과 의사소통하도록 해준다. 그것들은 매우 재미있다. 그러나, 당신이 그것들을 사용할 때 주의하지 않으면 그것들이 당신의 현실 생활에 문제를 일으킬 수도 있다.

소셜 네트워크 서비스를 이용할 때, 당신은 온라인에 게시한 것은 무엇이든지 항상 거기에 있을 것이라는 것을 기억해야 한다. 당신이 그것을 삭제하더라도, 다른 사람들이 그것을 복사하고, 저장하고, 전송하는 것은 쉽다. 게다가, 당신의 정보를 누가 보는지 결코 알 수 없다. 일단 당신이 그것을 온라인에 올리면, 그것은 공개적인 것이 된다. 부적절한 자료를 게시하는 것은 또한 당신에게 문제를 일으킬 수 있다. 실제로 당신은 온라인에 부적절한 내용을 게시한 것으로 심지어 체포될 수도 있다.

이런 일이 당신에게 일어나지 않도록 확실히 하기 위해서 당신이 취할 수 있는 몇 가지 조치들이 있다. 첫째로, 당신의 온라인 프로필을 비공개로 할 수 있다면, 그렇게 해야 한다. 이것은 당신이 누가 당신의 정보를 볼 수 있는지를 결정하게 할 것이다. 둘째로, 바른 온라인 예절을 갖춰라. 해가 되는 것들을 온라인상에서 말하거나 게시하지 마라. 좋은 규칙은 이것이다. 현실의 삶에서 하지 않을 일이라면, 온라인에서도 그것을 하지 말아라! 마지막으로, 당신이 이미 알고 있는 사람이 아니라면 절대로 온라인상에서의 친구를 실제로 만나는 것에 동의해서는 안 된다. 당신의 '친구'가 실제로는 당신에게 해를 끼치고 싶어 하는 사람일 수도 있다.

어휘

various 휑다양한   profile 명프로필, 인물 소개   post 동(인터넷에) 게시하다, 올리다   delete 동삭제하다   copy 동복사하다   save 동저장하다   inappropriate 휑부적절한   material 명물질; *자료   arrest 동체포하다   content 명내용   make sure 확실하게 하다   step 명걸음; *조치, 방법   private 휑사적인; *비공개의   etiquette 명예의, 에티켓   hurt 동다치게 하다; ~을 해치다   [문제] public 휑공공의; *공개적인   rumor 명소문   characteristic 명특성   avoid 동피하다   cautious 휑조심스러운, 신중한

구문 해설

7행   **When (you are) using** social networking services, you have to remember that *whatever* you post online will always be there.

- When과 using 사이에는 you are가 생략되어 있으며, 부사절의 주어가 주절의 주어와 같고 동사가 be동사일 때는 '주어 + be동사'를 생략할 수 있음
- whatever: ~한 것은 무엇이든 (= anything that)

14행   **To make sure** (that) this doesn't happen to you, there are some steps [(that) you can take].

- To make sure: '~하기 위해서'라는 의미로 목적을 나타내는 부사적 용법의 to부정사
- you can take 앞에는 목적격 관계대명사(that)가 생략됨

15행   This will **allow you to decide** *who can see your information.*

- allow + 목적어 + to-v: ~가 …하게 하다
- who 이하는 decide의 목적어 역할을 하는 간접의문문

Reading 2   p.74

⑤

해석

인터넷의 커지는 인기와 더불어, 사이버폭력이 심각한 문제가 되고 있다. (C) 사이버폭력은 위협하는 메시지를 보내거나 다른 사람의 비밀번호를 도용하는 것과 같이 어떤 형태로든 온라인상에서 괴롭히는 것이다. 그것은 다른 폭력 행위들보다 더 해로울 수 있다. (B) 이것은 괴롭히는 사람이 누구인지 찾아내는 것이 어려워서 사이버공간에서 괴롭히는 것이 훨씬 쉽기 때문이다. 또한 온라인상에서 괴롭히는 사람들은 그들의 피해자들에게 언제나, 어디서나, 심지어 집에서도 접근할 수 있다. (A) 게다가, 사이버폭력의 메시지는 아주 많은 사람들에게 빠르게 퍼진다. 사이버폭력을 멈추기 위해서 부모와 교사들은 그것이 얼마나 심각한지 이해해야만 한다. 그리고 당신이 괴롭힘을 당하고 있다면, 첫 번째로 해야 할 일은 누군가에게 (그것을) 이야기하는 것이다. 당신은 반드시 공개적으로 말하고 도움을 구해야 한다.

어휘

popularity 명인기   cyberbullying 명사이버폭력   spread 동퍼지다   bully 동괴롭히다 명괴롭히는 사람   speak out

거리낌 없이 말하다   victim ⑲피해자, 희생자   threatening ⑲위협하는   password ⑲비밀번호

구문 해설

5행   And if you're being bullied, the first thing to do is *to tell* someone.

- be being v-ed: 진행형 수동태
- to tell: '~하는 것'이라는 의미로 보어로 사용된 명사적 용법의 to부정사

7행   This is because bullying in cyberspace is **much** easier, as *it*'s difficult *to find out* who the bully is.

- much: '훨씬, 더욱'이라는 뜻으로 비교급을 강조하는 말 (또 다른 표현으로 a lot, far, even 등이 있음)
- it은 가주어, to find out 이하가 진주어임

Unit Review   p.75

A   [Reading 1] communicate, remove, private, manners   [Reading 2] victims

B   **1** various   **2** post   **3** etiquette   **4** rumor   **5** delete   **6** private

Reading 2 해석

사이버폭력은 괴롭히는 사람들이 쉽게 인터넷을 사용하여 피해자들을 크게 해치기 때문에 심각한 문제이다.

UNIT 18 *Entertainment*

Reading 1   pp.76-77

Before Reading   Yes, I saw that musical with my mom. It is about the friendship of two witches.

1 ②   **2** ④   **3** ①   **4** stands up for others and does her best to fight injustice in the land of Oz   **5** ④   **6** ③

해석

당신이 서쪽의 사악한 마녀인 엘파바를 영화 '오즈의 마법사'에서만 본 적이 있다면, 당신은 아마도 그녀가 정말 못된 인물이라고 생각할 것이다. 하지만 당신이 뮤지컬 '위키드'를 본다면, 당신은 그녀가 사실은 착한 마녀라는 것을 알게 되어 놀랄 것이다!

이 뮤지컬은 그레고리 매과이어의 소설에 기반을 둔다. 매과이어는 사람들이 엘파바 쪽의 이야기를 들어보기를 원했다. 이 뮤지컬의 저자는 그의 소설에 영감을 받았지만 그것을 정확하게 따르지는 않기로 결정했다. 대신 그녀는 엘파바의 밝혀지지 않은 이야기들과 글

린다와의 예상 밖의 우정에 초점을 맞췄다. 이 뮤지컬의 감동적인 줄거리와 기억에 남는 노래들 때문에, '위키드'는 수많은 주요한 상들을 받았고 계속해서 전 세계적으로 성공을 누리고 있다. (토니상은 매년 뛰어난 브로드웨이 공연에 주어진다.)

이 뮤지컬은 출생부터 대학에 가기까지, 그리고 많은 인생을 변화시키는 사건들을 통해 엘파바를 따라간다. 그리고 관람객들은 그녀의 초록색 피부 때문에 그녀가 항상 얼마나 불공평하게 판단되는지를 본다. 하지만 이야기가 전개됨에 따라, 그들은 엘파바가 좋은 사람이라는 것을 알게 된다. 그녀는 다른 사람들을 옹호하고 오즈의 나라에서 부당함에 맞서 싸우기 위해 최선을 다한다. 반면에, 관람객들은 선을 대표하는 글린다와 오즈의 마법사가 보이는 것처럼 친절하거나 현명하지 않다는 것을 알게 된다. 오즈의 비밀에 대해 더 많이 알게 되면서, 그들은 모든 이야기에는 항상 두 가지 면이 존재한다는 것을 깨닫는다.

어휘

witch ⑲마녀   wizard ⑲마법사   mean ⑲못된, 심술궂은   character ⑲성격, 기질; *등장인물   be based on ~에 근거하다[기초하다]   inspire ⑧영감을 주다   exactly ⑨정확히, 틀림없이   untold ⑲밝혀지지 않은   unlikely ⑲~할 것 같지 않은; *예상 밖의   moving ⑲감동시키는   storyline ⑲줄거리   memorable ⑲기억할 만한   major ⑲주요한, 중대한   award ⑲상   success ⑲성공   outstanding ⑲뛰어난   event ⑲사건, 일   viewer ⑲시청자, 관람객   judge ⑧판단하다, 평가하다   unfairly ⑨불공평하게   course ⑲강의; *추이, 전개   stand up for ~을 옹호하다   injustice ⑲불평등, 부당함   realize ⑧깨닫다, 알아차리다   [문제] wonder ⑲놀라움   impressive ⑲인상적인, 감명 깊은   worm ⑲벌레   feather ⑲깃털   flock ⑧모이다

구문 해설

1행   If you've only seen Elphaba, the Wicked Witch of the West, in the movie *The Wizard of Oz*, ...
  └──────┘ = └──────┘

15행   And the viewers see **how she is always judged unfairly because of her green skin**.
  • how 이하는 see의 목적어로 쓰인 간접의문문

Reading 2   p.78

②

해석

'위키드'에 관해 자주 묻는 질문들

질문 1: '위키드'는 얼마나 오래 공연하고 있는 중인가요?

'위키드'의 첫 공연은 뉴욕시에서 2003년 10월 30일에 있었습니다. 2022년 4월 24일 기준으로 그것의 7,082회의 공연은 '위키드'를 브로드웨이에서 5번째로 가장 오래 공연한 쇼로 만들었습니다! 이 쇼는 15분간의 휴식과 함께 약 2시간 30분 동안 지속됩니다.

질문 2: 그 쇼는 어떤가요?

'위키드'에는 토니상을 받은 아름다운 무대 장치들과 의상들, 그리고 여러분을 당장 오즈의 마법의 세계로 데려다줄 인상 깊은 노래들이 있습니다!

질문 3: 아이들이 '위키드'를 좋아할까요?

'오즈의 마법사'를 좋아하는 아이들은 '위키드'를 보는 것 또한 좋아합니다! 하지만 어린아이들을 위해 표를 구매하기 전에, 부모님들은 그 쇼의 공연 시간을 고려해야 합니다. 또한, 그 쇼에서 날아다니는 원숭이들은 일부 아이들을 무섭게 할지도 모릅니다. 하지만 전반적으로, 8세 이상의 아이들은 '위키드'를 마음에 든다고 생각할 것입니다.

frequently 🖭자주, 흔히   run 🖲(얼마의 기간 동안) 계속되다   performance 🖭*공연; 성과 (perform 🖲수행하다; *공연하다)   break 🖭휴식   set 🖭무대 장치[세트]   costume 🖭의상, 복장   transport 🖲수송하다; *(다른 장소나 시간으로) 데려다주다   magical 🖲마법의   in no time 당장에   take ~ into consideration ~을 고려하다   scare 🖲겁먹게[놀라게] 하다   in general 전반적으로   delightful 🖲정말 기분 좋은, 마음에 드는   [문제] scene 🖭장면

구문 해설

7행   ..., and impressive songs [**that** will transport you to the magical world of Oz in no time]!

· that은 impressive songs를 수식하는 주격 관계대명사

13행   ..., kids [**aged** eight and up] will *find Wicked delightful*.

· aged ... up은 kids를 수식하는 과거분사구
· find + 목적어 + 목적보어: ~을 …라고 여기다[생각하다]

Unit Review   p.79

A   Reading 1   novel, good, unfairly, fights, sides
B   **1** injustice   **2** character   **3** realize   **4** break   **5** memorable   **6** mean

Reading 1 해석

'위키드'는 그레고리 매과이어의 소설을 바탕으로 한 유명한 뮤지컬이다. 그것은 '오즈의 마법사'에 나오는 서쪽의 사악한 마녀인 엘파바의 이야기를 들려준다. 하지만 뮤지컬에서 엘파바는 착한 마녀로 드러난다. 그녀는 부당하게 대우받지만 다른 사람들을 옹호하고 부당함에 맞서 싸운다. 관람객들은 또한 선을 대표하는 글린다와 오즈의 마법사가 보이는 것처럼 친절하지 않다는 것을 알게 된다. 기억에 남는 노래와 줄거리를 통해 관람객들은 모든 이야기에는 항상 양면이 있다는 것을 알게 된다.

Before Reading I learned from a book that the first person in space was Yuri Gagarin.

1 ③   **2** ④   **3** ④   **4** made it easy for him to fit and move around in *Vostok 1*   **5** ①   **6** ③

해석

1961년 4월 12일에 소련은 인간을 우주에 보낸 최초의 국가가 되었다. 카자흐스탄의 사막으로부터 '보스토크 1호'라고 불리는 우주선이 별들을 향해 발사되었다. 비행은 108분간 지속되었는데, 이것은 지구를 한 바퀴 돌기에 충분히 긴 시간이었다. '보스토크 1호'는 지구 위로 200마일만큼 높이 도달했다.

보스토크의 조종사는 그가 관찰하는 모든 것을 기록해야 했다. 그러나 그는 비행 중 우주선에 대한 통제력이 없었다. 이는 우주에서 사람이 어떤 영향을 받게 될지 아무도 몰랐기 때문이다. 예를 들어, 우주의 낮은 중력은 조종사를 기절하게 했을 수도 있다. 그래서 우주선은 지상에서 통제되었다.

그렇다면 '우주의 콜럼버스'가 된 운이 좋은 사람은 누구였을까? 그것은 소련 공군의 소령인 유리 가가린이었다. 그는 부분적으로는 그의 체격 때문에 선발되었다고 알려져 있다. 그는 겨우 5피트(약 152cm)보다 조금 더 컸다. 이것은 그가 '보스토크 1호'에 맞게 들어가고 (그 안에서) 움직이는 것을 용이하게 했다. 또한 그의 다정하고 낙천적인 성격은 그가 역사적인 비행을 위한 고된 훈련을 견뎌 내는 데 도움이 되었다.

'보스토크 1호'의 성공은 더 많은 우주 프로그램들을 장려했고, 인간이 우주여행에서 살아남을 수 있다는 것을 보여주었다. 곧 더욱 많은 우주 비행사들이 우주로 여행한 사람들의 목록에 가가린과 함께 이름을 올렸다.

어휘

the Soviets 소련   desert 몡사막   spacecraft 몡우주선 (= craft)   launch 동(우주선 등을) 발사하다   record 동기록하다   control 몡동통제(하다)   flight 몡비행   gravity 몡중력   pass out 기절하다   ground 몡땅, 지면   get to-v ~하게 되다   major 몡소령   air force 공군   select 동선택하다, 뽑다   partly 閏부분적으로   fit 동(크기 등이) 맞다   easygoing 혱(성격이) 낙천적인, 원만한   go through ~을 겪다   historic 혱역사적으로 중요한   encourage 동권장하다, 촉진하다   survive 동~에서 살아남다   astronaut 몡우주 비행사   [문제] manned 혱(우주선 등이) 유인의   messenger 몡(문서 등의) 배달인; *전달자, 사신   cosmos 몡우주   height 몡키

구문 해설

4행   The flight lasted 108 minutes, **long enough to make** one circle around Earth.
- 형용사 + enough to-v: ~하기에 충분히 …한

5행   *Vostok 1* reached **as high as 200 miles** above Earth.
- as + 부사 + as A: A만큼 ~하게 (이때의 high는 부사로 '높이'의 의미임)

13행   **It is said that** he was selected partly because of his size.
- it is said that ~: ~라고들 한다

14행   This **made it easy** for him to fit and move around in *Vostok 1*.

가목적어   의미상 주어   진목적어

• make + 목적어 + 목적보어(형용사): ~을 …하게 만들다

Reading 2

④

해석

우주에서 무슨 냄새가 나는지 궁금해 본 적 있는가? 만약 여러분이 한 무리의 우주 비행사들에게 물어본다면, 그들은 그것이(우주가) 호두, 타 버린 스테이크, 또는 타는 금속 냄새가 난다고 말할지도 모른다. 그들은 우주 유영 후에 그들의 헬멧을 벗을 때마다 이런 이상한 냄새를 경험한다. 과학자들은 무엇이 이런 냄새의 혼합을 유발하는지에 대해 여전히 확신하지 못하지만, 그들은 몇 가지 이론들을 가지고 있다. 한 이론은 그 냄새들이 죽어가는 별들에서 나온다고 제안한다. 별들이 죽을 때, 그것들은 냄새나는 화학 물질의 혼합물을 우주에 방출한다. 이 화학 물질들은 우주를 떠돌고 다른 별들과 행성들의 생성에 관여한다. 그것들은 또한 지구에서 발견될 수 있고 우리가 기름, 석탄, 또는 심지어 음식을 태울 때도 종종 만들어진다.

어휘

wonder ⑧궁금해하다   walnut ⑲호두   burn ⑧태우다   metal ⑲금속   spacewalk ⑲우주 유영   mix ⑲혼합(물)   theory ⑲이론   suggest ⑧제안하다   chemical ⑲화학 물질   drift ⑧떠다니다   universe ⑲우주   take part in ~에 참여[참가]하다   creation ⑲생성   planet ⑲행성   coal ⑲석탄   [문제] release ⑧방출하다   smelly ⑱냄새 나는, 악취가 나는

구문 해설

1행   **Have** you ever **wondered** what space smells like?

• Have ~ wondered: '경험'을 나타내는 현재완료 시제

3행   They experience these strange smells **whenever** they take their helmets off after a spacewalk.

• whenever: ~할 때마다 (= every time)

Unit Review

A   **Reading 1**   human, launched, controlled, size   **Reading 2**   smell

B   **1** easygoing   **2** astronaut   **3** record   **4** wonder   **5** theory   **6** planet

Reading 1 해석

인간은 1961년 4월 12일에 처음으로 우주로 갔다. 그의 이름은 유리 가가린이었고 그는 '보스토크 1호'라고 불리는 소련의 우주선을 타고 여행했다. 그것은 카자흐스탄 사막으로부터 발사되었고 지구 위로 200마일을 날았다. 우주가 가가린에게 어떤 영향을 줄지 아무

도 알지 못했기 때문에, 우주선은 지상에서 통제되었다. 가가린이 그 역사적인 비행에 선발된 한 가지 이유는 그의 작은 체격이었는데, 이것은 그가 우주선 주변을 쉽게 움직이게 해주었다. 이후에, 많은 다른 사람들이 그 용감한 우주 비행사를 따라 우주로 갔다.

Reading 2 해석

일부 과학자들은 우주의 이상한 냄새가 죽어가는 별들에 의해 방출되는 화학 물질들에서 나온다고 믿는다.

UNIT 20 The Arts

Reading 1
pp.84-85

Before Reading I know his name and the painting *The Thinker*, as we learned about the work in our textbook.

1 ① **2** ② **3** wanted to honor the burghers **4** ② **5** ③ **6** (1) T (2) F

해석

백년전쟁 동안 영국군은 프랑스의 도시 칼레를 점령했다. 영국 왕은 만일 6명의 지도자, 즉 시민 대표들이 항복하고 목숨을 바친다면 그 도시의 사람들을 해치지 않겠다고 약속했다. 6명의 지도자는 자신들의 목숨을 포기하는 데 바로 동의했다. 이 행동을 통해 그 도시는 살아남았고, 왕은 그 용감한 사람들을 죽이지 않기로 결정했다.

500년 이상이 흐른 뒤인 1880년에 칼레 정부는 동상을 세워 그 시민 대표들을 기리기를 원했다. 그들은 그 계획을 위해 그 당시의 가장 유명한 조각가인 오귀스트 로댕을 고용했다. 그는 이후 10년 동안 그 동상 작업을 했다. 그러나 그가 드디어 끝마쳤을 때, 그 도시 지도자들은 별로 만족스러워하지 않았다. '칼레의 시민(The Burghers of Calais)'은 다른 어떤 동상과도 같지 않았다. 동상 속의 6인은 당당해 보이거나 영웅다워 보이는 대신, 피곤하고 걱정하는 듯이 보였다. 그것은 로댕이 그들의 진정한 감정을 보여 주길 원했기 때문이었다. 그는 그들이 아마도 자랑스러움을 느꼈으나 동시에 다가오는 죽음을 두려워했다고 생각했다. 또한, 그 동상은 대부분의 영웅 동상들이 그런 것처럼 높은 받침대 맨 위에 놓여 있지 않았다. 그것은 그것을 바라보는 사람들과 같은 높이에 있었다.

비록 로댕의 작품에 대해 많은 논쟁이 있었지만, 그것은 계속 칼레에 남았다. 오늘날 그것은 걸작이자 조각에서의 양식 변화의 중요한 예로 여겨지고 있다. 그 시민 대표들의 내면을 표현하고자 한 로댕의 노력은 오늘날에도 여전히 많은 예술가들에게 영감을 주고 있다.

어휘

army 몡*군대; 육군 capture 통붙잡다; *점령하다 surrender 통항복하다 right away 당장 honor 통~에게 경의를 표하다 statue 몡동상 hire 통고용하다 sculptor 몡조각가 (sculpture 몡조각) of the time 그 당시의 pleased 혱기쁜, 만족해하는 proud 혱자랑스러운, 당당한 heroic 혱영웅적인 (hero 몡영웅) afraid 혱두려워하는 base 몡기반, 토대 debate 몡논쟁, 토론 remain 통남다 masterpiece 몡걸작, 명작 [문제] tragic 혱비극적인 touching 혱감동적인 humorous 혱재미있는 mysterious 혱불가사의한 historical 혱역사상의 courageous 혱용기 있는 prevent 통막다

16행   It was at **the same** height **as** the people [*who* looked at it].

- the same A as B: B와 똑같은 A
- who 이하는 the people을 수식하는 주격 관계대명사절

18행   Today, it **is considered** ┌ a masterpiece
                                  │ and
                                  └ an important example of changing styles in sculpture.

- A is considered B: A는 B로 여겨지다 (consider A B의 수동태)

20행   Rodin's effort [**to show** the inner side of the burghers] is still inspiring ...

- to show는 Rodin's effort를 수식하는 형용사적 용법의 to부정사로 '～하기 위한, ～하려는'의 의미

Reading 2   p.86

②

해석

오귀스트 로댕은 1840년에 파리에서 태어났다. 그는 이른 나이에 예술에 관심을 갖게 되었지만, 조각가로서의 그의 이력은 순탄하지 않았다. 그는 예술 학교에 입학이 허가되지 않았고 장식용 돌 세공 일을 함으로써 가족을 부양해야 했다. 마침내 오랜 시간이 흐른 뒤, 사람들은 그가 얼마나 재능이 있는지 깨닫기 시작했다. 그의 걸작들은 '지옥의 문', '생각하는 사람' 그리고 '칼레의 시민'을 포함한다. 그의 조각들은 그것들의 힘과 사실성으로 유명하다. 그것들은 사람들의 열정과 연약함을 모두 보여 준다. 오늘날 로댕은 당대의 가장 훌륭한 조각가들 중 하나로 여겨진다.

어휘

career 몡경력, 이력   accept 동받아들이다   support 동부양하다   decorative 혱장식용의   stonework 몡돌 세공; 석조물   talented 혱재능 있는   hell 몡지옥   realism 몡사실주의, 리얼리즘   passion 몡열정   weakness 몡약점

구문 해설

3행   He ┌ was not accepted to art school
          │ and
          └ had to work **to support** his family *by doing* decorative stonework.

- to support: 목적을 나타내는 부사적 용법의 to부정사로 '～하기 위하여'의 의미
- by v-ing: ～함으로써

5행   Finally, after a long time, people began to realize **how talented he was**.

- how 이하는 realize의 목적으로 쓰인 간접의문문으로 '얼마나 ～인지'의 의미

A [Reading 1] statue, heroes, afraid, great   [Reading 2] challenges

B **1** honor   **2** sculptures   **3** passion   **4** heroic   **5** debate   **6** surrender

Reading 2 해석

비록 오귀스트 로댕은 그의 이력에서 많은 어려움들을 마주했지만 오늘날 그는 당대 최고의 조각가들 중 하나로 여겨진다.

MEMO

MEMO

JUNIOR
READING EXPERT

Level **4**